ALL ACROSS AMERICA, PEOPLE HAVE BEEN
STUNNED, MOVED, AND UPLIFTED BY
ROSEMARY ALTEA. DISCOVER WHY IN . . .
THE EAGLE AND THE ROSE

"I walked through the front door of where Ms. Altea has been
staying a skeptic, my purse empty of handkerchiefs and tissues.
I walked out two and a half hours later, leaving dozens of sopping wet tissues behind. . . . Maybe I had become a believer."
—ELAINE LOUIE, *New York Times*

"On national television, Rosemary Altea rendered Larry King
speechless with a personal message from his long-dead mother;
at a bookstore in San Francisco, she stunned a recent widow by
announcing that the woman's late husband was standing right
behind her. 'He thanks you for the rose,' Altea said. 'I laid a
rose in his coffin just before the burial,' said the woman. 'Now,
how could you know that?'"
—ALIX MADRIGAL, *San Francisco Chronicle*

"People who believe the dead are always with us will be fascinated by THE EAGLE AND THE ROSE."
—*USA Today*

Please turn this page for more
praise for THE EAGLE AND THE ROSE

"A riveting story. [It] calls upon each of us to remember that we live in a theater of souls much grander than outer appearances."

—JOAN BORYSENKO, PH.D., author of *Fire in the Soul*

"A moving account. The author's simplicity and patent sincerity will warm the hearts of readers who reserve judgment in spiritualist phenomena. Here is the heroic story of Rosemary Altea's 'blossoming' into life and establishing centers where people can receive spiritual and psychic healings."

—*Kirkus Reviews*

"I was completely captivated."

—WILLIS HARMAN, president, Institute of Noetic Sciences, and author of *Global Mind Change*

"Rosemary Altea's stunning account of the existence of life after death brings us right up to the frontier of evolutionary advancement. The message in THE EAGLE AND THE ROSE is multilayered—serving our human needs for connection to loved ones and stimulating our spirit of adventure to cross the bridge between two planes of existence."

—CAROL ADRIENNE, coauthor of *The Celestine Prophecy: An Experiential Guide*

THE EAGLE
and
THE ROSE

A Remarkable True Story

ROSEMARY ALTEA

WARNER BOOKS

A Time Warner Company

WARNER BOOKS EDITION

Copyright © 1995 by Rosemary Altea
All rights reserved.

Warner Books, Inc., 1271 Avenue of the Americas, New York, NY 10020

Visit our Web site at www.twbookmark.com.

For information on Time Warner Trade Publishing's online program, visit www.ipublish.com.

 A Time Warner Company

Printed in the United States of America
Originally published in hardcover by Warner Books, Inc.
First Trade Printing: July 2001

The Library of Congress has cataloged the hardcover edition as follows:
Altea, Rosemary.
    The Eagle and the Rose: a remarkable true story / Rosemary Altea.
        p.   cm.
    ISBN 0-446-51969-3
    I. Altea, Rosemary. 2. Women mediums—Biography. 3. Future life—Miscellanea.
4. Grey Eagle (Spirti) I. Title
BF1283.A58A3   1995
133.9'092—dc21   94-42252
[B]   CIP

ISBN-13: 978-0-446-67778-3

Book design by Giorgetta Bell McRee
Cover design by Julia Kushnirsky
Cover illustration by Jan Francois Podevin

To my daughter Samantha.
First in my life, she is my light . . . my miracle

Do you love me, or do you not . . .
You told me once, and I forgot . . .

Acknowledgments

I would like to thank all those wonderful people who have helped me . . . who have shared my journey. Friends, dear friends, and colleagues, far too many to mention but whose names are written on my heart.

Dear friends without whose support I could not have written this book.

You who will know, will know that I thank you. That Grey Eagle thanks you.

To Kay. To Pat. To Lynne and Peter. To Claire. And to my friend and confidante Joan, goes my deepest gratitude, and my love.

My thanks also to my personal assistant Perrin Read, who brings light and organization to an otherwise cluttered world.

My deepest gratitude to my editor Joann Davis, whose help in writing this book has been invaluable.

And to Joni Evans my agent and my friend. . . . a feather!

We are not human beings having a spiritual experience.
We are spiritual beings having a human experience.

—PIERRE TEILHARD DE CHARDIN

Contents

PART I

The Awakening

Peter

I was in Whitby, a coastal resort in the north of England. It was a warm summer night, and although it was quite late, the small holiday town was busy. Gangs of youths had been arriving since early summer, looking for work, and unable to find any, they had become a bit of a problem for the locals.

As I stood watching one such gang, a rowdy but good-natured lot, I was aware of a couple of police cars placed strategically along the main street, obviously on the alert in case of trouble. Although there wasn't much traffic, the lads were pushing each other into the road as the occasional car passed through.

One boy among them, the daredevil of the group, would leap out in front of every passing car, sometimes coming within inches of being hit, laughing and shouting at the poor motorist, with a catch-me-if-you-can attitude.

You might easily reach the conclusion that this boy had a

death wish, or perhaps he believed that death only happened when one was old.

The police, not wishing to cause any more trouble than necessary, watched and waited, hoping the group would eventually get tired of their game and drift off home.

Heading toward the center of Whitby was Peter, who had just landed a job with a marine company. Overjoyed with the news, he had arranged to meet his sister and two friends for a celebratory dinner. The evening turned out to be a great success, but all too soon Peter and his friends were saying their good-byes. The three young men piled into Peter's little car and set off toward the town center.

Standing in the street, still watching this gang of high-spirited youths playing their game, dicing with death, I noted that with each escape they were becoming more rowdy and more careless.

As Peter's car approached, I saw the headlights, clear and bright, lighting up the street. The young and silly daredevil, waiting until the very last minute, leapt out into the road. I knew instinctively that he was about to get his death wish.

Peter realized too late what was happening and tried to spin the car away from the figure looming large in front of him. But the car hit the boy and sent him spinning onto the pavement, where he fell, his head crashing onto the hard surface. It was this blow, and not the impact of the car, that killed him.

The horror of the accident written plainly on his pale countenance, Peter panicked. Putting his foot down hard on the accelerator, he sped out of the town center, making for the cliff road.

A police car chased after him, and as I followed Peter's car

I could hear, quite clearly, his two pals yelling at him, begging him to stop.

Soon, bringing his car to a standstill, with the police car pulling up alongside, Peter scrambled out and began running up on to the cliff path.

His friends, desperate, shouted, "Peter, don't. Come back! Please, Peter, come back!"

I watched as this tall, good-looking young man, his blond hair standing out starkly in the night, raced along the cliff top, the policeman hot on his heels. His two pals, now sobbing uncontrollably, hung on to each other, helpless, frightened, and bewildered by the events that had taken place. But my attention was brought back to the two figures running along the cliff top, and I heard the policeman, breathless and tired, call out, "Please stop, lad, please."

But Peter ran on. Suddenly, approaching a clump of bushes and too weary to run any farther, he dived behind them.

The young officer had seen Peter hiding and slowed his step. Cautiously he advanced toward the shrubbery and in a low, soft voice tried to persuade Peter to give himself up.

For a few seconds I thought he would succeed, as Peter stood up and made toward the policeman, but then the policeman took a step forward, and Peter shot back into the bushes.

There was a loud scream, and I saw the handsome young man with the blond hair topple and fall over the edge of the cliff.

His lean body seemed to hang in space for a brief second before it crashed onto the rocks below. The bushes that Peter had hidden behind had themselves been hiding the cliff edge.

•   •   •

The scene that I had witnessed with horror and shock now shifted in front of my eyes and became misty. Suddenly I was back in my study in Epworth, a small town in the north of England, where I lived, and the lady sitting before me was crying as I recounted all that I had seen.

The atmosphere in my little room was tense and filled with sadness, and I had begun to wonder what I could do to help my client cope with the awful burden she had to carry, when I heard his voice again. This time it was clear and sharp and directed at me. I turned to where I thought the voice had come from, and a young man chuckled. "Not over there, silly," he said. "I'm over here, next to Gran. Can't you see me yet?"

I looked to where my client sat, a large, comfortable lady in her late sixties, but still I couldn't see him.

Laughing now, I said, "Come on, Peter, stop playing games. I haven't got time for them this afternoon." Immediately I saw a handsome young man, slim and very fair, a delighted grin on his face, standing next to my client's chair.

Placing his hand on her shoulder, Peter said proudly, "This is my gran, you know. Isn't she lovely?"

When I repeated this comment to "Gran," she burst into tears again and, sobbing, said over and over again, "Oh, Peter. Oh, Peter. Why did you have to leave me?"

Peter, completely unperturbed by this, said, "She keeps on saying that all the time, and she just won't stop crying. D'you think you could make her understand that I'm okay? Tell her that I am having a great time here, and that Gramps is with me now."

Again I relayed the message that Peter had given, and, as I mentioned Gramps I saw a tall, stoutly built gentleman, who gave his name as Paul, and confirmed that he was indeed Peter's grandfather.

"I passed over just a year after Peter," he told me. "I'd been having trouble with my heart, you know, and Peter's accident, or the shock of it, just finished me off."

Well, of course, I didn't know and had to ask my client if she understood what Paul had said. She was able to verify that Paul was her husband and Peter her grandson, telling me how close they all had been and how she had felt, since Peter's accident, that the rest of the family had somehow drifted apart.

There were many things said that first memorable sitting, and my client confirmed with a nod of her head every detailed piece of evidence given.

Paul was keen to talk about the family business that he and his wife had built up together over the years and which was now being run by his two capable sons. He wanted his wife to let them know that he was still around and still taking an interest in things.

Occasionally, though, Peter and his grandfather would start up a conversation between themselves and I would have to remind them that they were supposed to be talking to me.

My impressions of Peter, after our first meeting, were that he is a very likable and intelligent young man with a tremendous zest for life. Full of fun and extremely quick-witted, he keeps me on my toes every time I meet him, which is quite often, as his gran has been back to see me quite a few times.

The one thing that strikes me, more than anything else, about this lovely young man is that he has an amazing capacity for expressing joy, and because he has such a positive attitude about life, he has adapted to his new mode of living remarkably well. The sun shines in my little study every time Peter comes through to talk to me, although there is one small shadow in his life.

For Peter's father, there is no life after death, and the tragedy of his son's passing stays, buried, deep within his heart. He rarely talks about his son, the pain is too deep, and Peter has told me that his father believes that "when you're dead, you're dead," and nothing can ever change that fact.

Peter knows that to get his father to understand that he is still very much alive is not going to be easy. In fact, as Peter puts it, "It's going to take a hammer and chisel to get through my father's thick skull that there is such a thing as life after death." Still, he insists he'll keep on trying.

Even as I have been writing Peter's story, I know that this wonderful and sensitive young man has been beside me, making sure that I get every detail right. Because he is the kind of young man who just refuses to admit defeat in all things, and also because for the last five minutes I haven't been able to shut him up, I am going to allow him to have the last word.

"Dad, I am here, honestly I am, and I love you, Peter XXX."

The
Beginning

When Peter's grandmother came to see me I had been working as a medium for several years. For me, Peter's story was not an unusual one. I had spoken often before to others in the spirit world, had heard many sad tales, witnessed the pain and heartache of the bereaved, and had observed their struggle to deal with their loss. I had experienced many other extraordinary things as well, including out-of-body travel, trance work, and the rescue of lost souls. But wait, I am getting too far ahead of myself. How did it begin . . . how far back must we go as I attempt to unfold the mystery that is my gift, my oh so precious gift?

According to my mother, I have been odd since I was a small child—so much so that she was at times convinced I would end up in the local mental hospital as a patient.

Her reasons for thinking this were, I suppose, quite valid. Having five other children—two boys and three girls—who were in her eyes quite normal, I must have seemed very different, and I know that she found me difficult to understand, and perhaps even more difficult to love. She had a quick temper and a cruel tongue, and because I was so unlike the others I was often made the scapegoat.

Her marriage to my father was a miserable and unhappy one, so there were always traumas or difficulties of one sort or another, and she would often vent her anger on me.

We lived in the Midlands, in the city of Leicester, in a small council house on the wrong side of town. This is where I was born and raised, a year after the Second World War ended, and where I grew up. From my early childhood, from the very beginnings of my life, I can remember seeing faces in the night, unrecognizable and terrifying. They appeared to loom out of the darkness and hover over me in what seemed then a very menacing way. I would hear voices muttering but never quite understand what they were saying. Sometimes the faces seemed so awful, and frighteningly large, in brilliant Technicolor, that I would cry out and my mother would once again have to deal with this awkward child.

My father, a demanding and unreasonable bully with a temper made worse by my mother's constant nagging and moaning, was a professional soldier who had been in the army most of his adult life. This meant that he was away from home for most of my childhood until I was eleven years old, returning only on weekends and holidays, leaving my mother to raise six children. Not an easy task for any mother, but ours had a job working nine A.M. to six P.M. in a factory, folding and packing carbon paper. Because of my mother's income, we were the only kids in our neighborhood who went on vacation every year. Our house displayed fitted carpets and brocade curtains. Very posh.

I can still remember "bath nights"—Sundays—before modern plumbing was installed. In the corner of the kitchen was a large copper boiler and just above it the dreaded pump. The "copper," as it was called, had to be filled with water and heated. Then my mother would stand at the pump, working the handle up and down for what seemed like hours, until the bath upstairs was filled with hot water, after which she would haul me and my sisters in one at a time.

God forbid that any of us cried if she scrubbed too hard, which she often did in her frustration, because we would then feel her hand across our bare backsides. And boy, did my mother have hard hands! Tired out, and with patience exhausted by six children, my mother would feel relieved when she had bathed us and tucked us into bed and could put her feet up for what was left of the evening.

I am certain that we could have survived quite well on my father's salary, but my mother wanted to do more than just survive. Her home and our holidays kept her going, but everything has its price, and all the comfort in the world doesn't spell happiness.

I cannot remember ever sitting on my mother's knee or being loved in any way. My childhood memories do not include those of affection and warmth, only loneliness and rejection and fear, real fear. I was a timid and nervous child, never sure, never trusting, always needing. And there was one more thing, an added worry: Was I like my grandmother?

I never met my maternal grandmother, as she passed over when I was only six weeks old, nor have I ever "seen" or "spoken" to her in my capacity as a medium. She was only in her early fifties when one day she collapsed and died, apparently without warning. Her name was Eliza, and although I have never seen a photograph of her, I am told that I look very much like her. My mother was her only child, and from tales that I have been told, Eliza must have had a difficult time bringing her up. My mother was, as a child and as an adult, a very strong-willed and determined person.

But Eliza had another problem, one that must have seemed too great to overcome. She thought she was mad.

Grandmother Eliza used to hear voices whispering in her ear and all around her. Voices of people who weren't there. Voices, but no people. These voices would speak to her—and only her, for nobody else could hear them. So persistent were they, so clear, and so afraid did Eliza become, that she signed herself voluntarily into the local psychiatric hospital—The Towers, in the middle of Leicester.

How often she had treatment for her mental state I don't know. I do know that not only was Eliza convinced that she was on occasions mentally deranged, but my mother was of the same opinion.

Now, here I was, a young girl with what? A vivid imagination? Perhaps seeing faces or hearing voices was my way of getting attention, or could it be that in addition to my grandmother's features I had inherited her madness? Even as I write this passage I can still hear my mother's voice screaming at me—whenever she was frustrated because I hadn't perhaps behaved "normally," or when I had done something that was, to her way of thinking, "strange"—"You'll end up like your grandma . . . in The Towers!"

Although this was said partly as a threat to make me "behave," I think my mother believed I would indeed end up in this notorious mental hospital. Even as I grew older and learned not to tell people about the things I saw and heard, my mother's suspicions about my state of mind remained with me. The threat of madness was there, always in the back of my mind.

It is true that things said often enough, particularly in childhood, stay with you for the rest of your life, and my mother's words, "You'll end up like your grandma," were to haunt me for a very long time. Whenever something strange or inexplicable happened, this specter of madness would rear its head. It was only my involvement with my church and my belief in God and in Jesus Christ that helped me hold on to my sanity. There were many times in my life that those dreaded fingers of fear would clutch my heart and squeeze tight, taking my breath and making me believe that I must surely be insane.

Growing up was torture, always being afraid, never daring to tell, and, naturally shy and sensitive, I grew timid and more nervous as the years passed.

At sixteen I fell in love. My John was twenty-two, gentle, loving, and a dream come true. We were engaged to be married on my seventeenth birthday. My father disliked him intensely and had thought in the beginning that as I was so young the relationship would fizzle out. It didn't. But then one year after we were engaged my father banned John from the house and made our lives together impossible.

John had been my protector, my strength. Now I was alone and afraid again. Afraid of my "gift," afraid of my father, afraid of life.

I was nineteen years old when I met and married my husband, a man my father approved of. He seemed stable, secure. He told me the things I needed to hear—and he seemed also to be my best means of escape. I couldn't have been more wrong.

Still I hadn't told him or anyone of my gift, not even John, whom I had loved dearly, still loved; still I had explained to no one about my visions and voices, those voices that would come to me in the night.

Less than one week after I was married, I discovered my husband had taken a girlfriend to bed just two days before the wedding. That set the scene for the next fourteen years, and although there were some happy times, I knew that I had escaped one emotional prison for another.

In my early thirties, with a ten-year-old daughter, many things in my life had changed. I had been deserted—perhaps "abandoned" is more exact—by my husband, who believed that responsibilities were all right as long as they weren't his. Responsibilities included me, our daughter, the house, financial affairs, and so on.

In all those years, I had never spoken to him of my experiences with the spirit world, or of my fears concerning my sanity. I had worked so hard and for so long to live a "normal" life, to be a "normal" human being. I just wanted to "fit in," to be like everyone else, and had I talked to him or anyone else of my gift, which to me at that time was not a gift but a curse, I would have been admitting to them that I was not normal at all, but some kind of freak. Many times while I was married I would wake in the night, shaking and terrified and needing the light on, having had yet another scary "nightmare," but only one time in all the years that we were together did my husband witness more than this.

I had arranged a small dinner for my husband's boss— they were in the fashion business—and a friend of mine, Susan, who made up the foursome. It was a simple affair, relaxed and easy. I had known Maxwell, my husband's employer, for some time, and this was not the first time he had been to our home. It was over coffee that he began to tell a story, unbidden by the rest of us, of how a few years earlier he had visited by chance a "spiritualist" church. He told how he had stood at the back of a small room filled with people, strangers he had never met before, and how a man at the front of the crowd had pointed him out and told Maxwell of his life and of his grandfather, and how he had revealed some of the more intimate details of Maxwell's life that no one there could possibly have known.

We listened, intrigued but skeptical of his story. Then he turned his attention to me. "Do you believe in life after death?" he asked.

Wary, but wanting without knowing it to talk, I said very carefully, "Yes, I do."

"Do you believe that someone is watching over and protecting your three-year-old daughter?" Maxwell then asked.

Again, warily, I answered that I did, and when he asked me who I thought that this might be, I replied that it could possibly be my husband's grandfather who was taking care of my child.

With that he jumped up from the table and asked for a pack of cards. He took hold of my hand and led me into the sitting room, my husband and friend following, and told me that he could help me find out who my daughter's "guide" might be. Now I was nervous, but Maxwell was my husband's boss, a guest in my home, and I was naturally respectful toward him. I allowed him to continue with what I thought was his silly game.

He sat me down at one end of the sofa, and he sat opposite me at the other end. In one hand he held the pack of cards and in the other he held my husband's grandfather's wedding ring, which he had asked my husband for. As I watched, now quite intrigued, Maxwell cut the cards and placed the two halves of the pack facedown, side by side, and then he placed the wedding band between the cards and just in front.

"Now," he said, glancing up at me, "I want you to concentrate hard on the ring. There will be on the top of these"—he tapped both piles of cards with his finger—"either a jack, a king, or a queen. The ring," he continued, "will tell you which pile to choose, and if, when you have chosen, the top card is a king or a jack, you will know that it is a male spirit who watches over your daughter. If, on the other hand, I turn up a queen, well then, that will tell you that there is a female spirit, possibly a grandmother, who watches over your child. Concentrate on the ring," he said again, "and it will show you which pile of cards to choose."

I thought he was mad. I had never heard such rubbish. Did he really expect us to believe this, or was it a joke, an elaborate hoax, and I the unknowing "straight man"? Well, I thought, he's the boss, so just humor him. So it was with these thoughts that I looked at the ring.

Only seconds passed . . . and the ring moved. I blinked my eyes shut—imagination, I told myself—and opened my eyes again. Seconds passed and again the ring moved . . . or seemed to move, over to the left. This is ridiculous, I thought, angry with myself for getting caught up in Maxwell's drama. Then the ring moved again, and before I knew what was happening I was caught up in a drama all of my own. Something, some power, had seized hold of my body, and a huge weight seemed to be crushing down on me, pushing me down into the sofa. I was paralyzed, just couldn't move, couldn't escape this tremendous force, but my mind was screaming out in sheer terror. Slowly then, very slowly, it began . . . that creeping feeling I had had so many times before when, as a child and as an adult, I had lain terrified, unable to move, as some unseen force tried to pull my face away from me. I sat on the sofa, tears pouring down my face, unable to move, even to blink, trying desperately to lift my hands to my face to protect myself, screaming in my head, God help me, please someone help me!

My husband and our friend Susan had both leapt up from their chairs and rushed to help me even though I had uttered not one sound; they had watched as my face had drained completely of color, and my distress was obvious to them. Maxwell's arm shot out, his voice commanding that I not be touched.

I could see and hear all of this even as I sat, my terror mounting, as the terrible weight seemed to increase and push me down even farther. Maxwell's voice was coming across to me, quietly but insistent, trying to reassure me that I was all right, that he would help me . . . but the truth was that he was totally out of his depth. Nothing like this had ever happened to him before, but he remained calm, although my husband was yelling at Maxwell to "do something." I was totally involved now with my own struggle as I tried yet again to lift my hands to my face, which seemed to be being peeled off like a mask. Then, just as suddenly as it had begun, the force was gone. The pressure left me and my hands flew to my face. Now I was so scared that I really cried. Susan fetched me a drink, and slowly I forced myself to "feel" normal. Maxwell took me for a walk around the garden, and the fresh night air brought me round and I felt so much better. But when I went back indoors and everyone wanted to talk about what had happened, I was so scared that I just could not bring myself to tell them. Twice more during that same evening I momentarily had that awful creeping sensation, as if my face were slowly being peeled away, and I just burst into tears.

My husband, Maxwell, and Susan had all been witness to an unexplainable and paranormal experience. They had all noticed that the temperature had dropped and the atmosphere in the room had changed dramatically during the hour that this event had taken place. The next morning Susan called to see if I was okay and told me how strange I had looked and how scared she had been; but apart from that one time neither she, Maxwell, nor my husband ever mentioned the incident again. It was brushed away, too difficult to deal with, too scary to contemplate, and the possibilities of what "it" might have been, oh no . . . no one in his right mind would ever want to consider.

And of course, it could just be that I was more than a little crazy, more like Grandma Eliza, than I dared think. When would it be my turn . . . when would they take me for treatment . . . when would my inherited madness be discovered? Never, I resolved, never; so I too swept the incident away, along with all the others that I had had over the years. It was just a game that had gone badly wrong, and I was never to talk about it again . . . until much later—much, much later, several years, in fact. And it was even later still when I came to understand what it had all meant.

After fourteen years of my husband's womanizing and continual financial messes, I was driven to seek a divorce. Not being able to understand that I had simply had enough of a one-sided marriage, he swore that he would see me starve before he paid me a penny to support either me or Samantha, our daughter.

He very nearly succeeded ... but not quite. We didn't starve, but it was no thanks to him.

There are many kinds of loneliness in the world, but living with someone and being lonely is for me the worst kind. To lie in bed next to somebody and not be able to reach out and touch that person, not to talk or share the little things in life, seems a worse fate than having no one at all.

One day I came home to find him gone, and the money with him. All that was left of this tattered relationship was a string of debts and a ten-year-old child. The debts took years to settle and caused me much worry and heartache, but it was worth it just to be free at last. Although at one time I must have loved this man, to be rid of the weight of unrest and insecurity caused by his lying and cheating was wonderful.

My now ex-husband kept his word about not supporting us, and neither my daughter nor I have seen or heard from him since that time.

But I am the lucky one. Samantha and I have a very special and close relationship, and there is a tremendous feeling of love and affection between us. If I had to go through the pain and sadness of that time again in order to have my daughter, I would do it gladly.

So living now in the north of England, where I had moved with my husband some five or so years earlier, I found life was by no means easy. I was an emotional wreck, everything seemingly in tatters around my feet, and struggling financially. On top of all that, my visions, voices, and strange sensations, which had followed me through my life, started to become more vivid and to occur more frequently than before. I was once sitting alone in the living room at home, reading a book, when I looked up to see a man sitting opposite me on the settee. He didn't say a word, just stared at me intently. I heard myself talking to him, quite naturally, and remember thinking later that I must be mad. I knew that he was what some would call a ghost, even though he looked just like you or me and not as one would imagine a ghost to look. No wispy bits around the edges, not a bit pale or illuminated, just very ordinary. I knew with that telling instinct born to me that he was of another world, not because of his looks, but because of a recognition I find impossible to describe, the recognition of a soul free of earthly restrictions, of a soul born free.

Another time I woke up in bed to find two strangers, men of the spirit world but so real they could have been burglars, standing just inside the bedroom door. Again, not a word was said; they just looked at me. I scrambled up, struggling in my terror for the bedside lamp, which I switched on. When I looked back they were gone, and I was left shaking and alone.

My terrible fear of the dark stems from my childhood experiences. I still remember how I would hide underneath the bedclothes, sweating and trembling with fear, to escape from those awful faces. My mother refused to give in to what she considered to be my overactive imagination, and never did she allow me the comfort of a light. I was never to recognize those faces; never to know if they were the same or different each time; never to recognize the voices, whispering, calling; never to understand what was being said or what they wanted. I could only pray that they would go away. After I left home I always slept with a light to comfort me.

This particular night, when my two "visitors" came, the

landing light was on and the bedroom door was ajar. But instead of the light giving me a feeling of security and comfort, it seemed to add a ghostly glow to the whole scene, and I was really scared. I remember scrambling around in the direction of the bedside table, trying to locate the lamp, which I knew was there . . . somewhere. When I eventually found it and switched it on, the men had disappeared and I was left all alone, wondering, Was it a dream? In my heart of hearts I knew that it had been much too real, that I hadn't been dreaming. I lay awake for the rest of the night, terrified that "they" might be back—and what then?

Many times I have been awakened in the early morning hours, experiencing a sensation I can only describe as a feeling of having two faces—as if I were wearing a mask that someone, or something, was attempting to pry from my face. The physical sensations are so real as to make my face seem misplaced or lopsided. Always I was left shaking and terrified.

From childhood to adulthood I lived with uncertainty, never knowing when the shadows would loom close or if they would overtake me. No matter how much I tried to understand what was happening to me, I was confused. No matter how much I then tried to ignore these strange visitations and happenings, I couldn't.

I grew up in two worlds, one a world of ghosts and specters, as real as I was, the other a world where what was real was always something you could explain, or touch or see and show others so that they too could see. One world was terrifying, the other cruel and unhappy.

I can remember as a child my mother saying, about herself, quite often and usually from sheer frustration, "I must be going mad! " I know that many people, including myself, have used the same expression either in jest or frustration or perhaps for some other reason. One thing I found during this strange and lonely period of my life was this: If you genuinely believed, as I did, that you really were cracking up, that your mental state was such that someone might just turn up to "put you away," that you were in fact "going crazy," you didn't tell a soul!

I was now thirty-four years old, and from the first time I can remember I had been "haunted." Real or not real, debate as you will, I was caught up in a dimension of life that exceeded that which was considered by most as normal. Afraid and alone in my confusions, misunderstood and misunderstanding, my reality was different from that of anyone I knew, my judgments clouded and my sanity definitely in question.

Now on top of all else, my husband had disappeared. Apart from my youngest sister, my family was totally nonsupportive as I struggled to raise my daughter. My state benefit was low, and I was forced for a while to work part-time behind a bar, where I had to ward off the constant and unwanted attentions of the lecherous landlord until I could not stand it any longer and left.

With a very limited education, having left school at age fifteen to work in a ladies' dress shop, I had no job qualifications and no time to go back to school or train for anything. The year was 1980, my daughter was now ten years old, and I was not yet divorced, as no one could find my husband. I was separated and "crazy" . . . most definitely, to my mind, *crazy*.

I found myself becoming more and more introverted, hiding my true self from everyone. I put on an act to fool people and pretended that I was quite happy and "normal," but the strain of this soon began to show. I stopped going out of the house, even to the village shops. When I had to buy food I would go to the nearest town where nobody knew me, and that way I didn't have to put on any false smiles or pretend that everything was all right. It wasn't. I became a virtual recluse. Only two things were important to me. One was that my daughter remain happy and secure. I felt that she needed to see me as strong and stable, and it took all of my efforts to give her that security. Second, I was determined no one would separate us, take my daughter from me.

I had been on my own for a few months when one day a friend who had been watching me going steadily downhill decided to take action. She phoned and said, "You are coming out with me tonight. There is someone local advertising a talk on tarot cards. Not just a talk, but a demonstration as well."

I told her that I wasn't going, but she insisted that I was, and because she is a very forceful and somewhat bossy lady, I knew it was pointless to argue with her. I simply said, "I'm not going," and put down the phone.

At seven o'clock that evening a knock came at the door, and there she was. Pushing her way into the house, she declared, "You've stayed in long enough, and I'm not leaving without you."

Luckily, although I didn't think so at the time, Samantha was staying overnight with one of her friends, so I had no reason or excuse not to go out. I felt a tremendous resentment at Jean's intrusion into my life, but at the same time an odd sense of relief that I wasn't going to spend the evening alone.

Still, I was reluctant to face the world or to meet people

I didn't know and to whom I might have to speak. They might sense that I was strange. As I have already said, someone who believes that they are going mad tries to appear quite normal and is frightened in case anyone suspects otherwise.

So here I was, going to a stranger's house and having to mix with people whom I had never met before. Any thoughts as to what sort of evening it was to be never crossed my mind. Only one thing was important, and this was that they—these strangers—mustn't learn the truth about me.

All the way in the car I sat silent and brooding, feeling that this private little world I had built up for myself so carefully over the last few months was being invaded. Eventually we pulled up in front of a small white cottage, standing alone in what at first seemed like acres of a no-man's-land. Having driven down some long rutted country lanes, which were really no more than dirt tracks, to find ourselves in this wilderness was a bit of a surprise, not at all what I had expected.

I was told later that this place, called the Turbary, was a sort of nature reserve, which accounted for the air of desolation and lack of buildings.

Jean and I were met at the door by Irene and Paul Denham, a retired couple who owned the place. She was in her mid-fifties, short and dark, quite attractive; he was in his sixties, taller and quite distinguished looking. The Denhams invited us in and introduced us to what seemed to me quite a crowd of people. There were actually only about a dozen other guests, but the room in which we had all been seated was quite small and therefore seemed overcrowded.

I was placed on the only empty chair left in the room,

next to a small table, behind which was seated a slim, dark young man perhaps in his late twenties. I guessed he was the speaker. Because I was seated next to him, I felt quite conspicuous and can remember pushing myself back as far as I could go onto the chair in an effort to make myself seem smaller.

There was a lot of small talk going on, everyone chatting to each other; a very friendly atmosphere was being created, and some there were obviously excited and intrigued by what was about to be discussed.

Now at that time I knew nothing about tarot cards other than that they had little pictures on them and that some people believed in using them to tell the future. I don't know much more than that even now, except that it is a subject I prefer to leave alone and something I now would advise others to be very careful and critical of. It is not the cards that I am wary of, but the ability of the reader.

Eventually the speaker, whose name was John, was introduced to us all, and the demonstration began. First he gave a talk, explaining how long tarot cards had been in use and the meanings of the pictures. Each card, he said, was different, and although a card placed on its own had one meaning, putting it with a few others in the pack could completely change the interpretation. Basically what happens is that a few cards are placed face up on the table, in a certain pattern. Someone adept at understanding the cards can then, by interpreting them "correctly," gain a certain knowledge concerning the person being read.

Now if you will remember, I had not been at all happy about going out and was not really in the right frame of mind to listen to all this. I was too busy trying to stay inconspicuous. So most of what this young man was saying went over my head.

Then he told us he was going to give a demonstration, and he began, one by one and quite slowly, to lay down the cards, face up, on the table in front of him. Because I was seated so close to him, it was impossible not to watch. I could see every card as it was placed, and my eyes became riveted to the table.

The strange but now familiar feeling began to creep over me that I was not myself, and I could do nothing but accept it. I knew for certain, sensed, that those cards were being dealt out for me. More than that, I knew exactly what they meant. They told of my life as it was now. Of the confusion and pain.

Suddenly, almost as if he were reading my mind, John turned to me and, looking straight into my eyes, said: "These cards have been laid out for you."

I sat there, amazed, not daring to say a word, and I believed that he knew that I was crazy. But these were my thoughts, not his. He then turned back to the rest of the group and continued his explanation of the demonstration. I could feel panic rising inside me and thought, He's going to tell them—he's going to tell them about me. But he didn't, he didn't say a word, and soon after he ended his talk and sat down.

We were then told that after a cup of tea a group discussion was to follow. All I could think of was that I must get home, get out of there, before John let the cat out of the bag. Jean, of course, would have none of it.

"We're staying," she said. "Don't be such a wet blanket."

As soon as the teacups were cleared away, Paul Denham, the host, brought the group to order. He suggested that perhaps there were people present who had themselves been for a tarot reading.

"Or maybe," he said, "there is someone here who has firsthand experience of the paranormal?"

Of course, there is always someone in a group like this who has perhaps seen a ghost, or knows someone who has. In no time at all people began recounting stories, either their own or one a friend had told them. Everyone seemed to have something to say on the subject. Tarot cards were forgotten, as one by one tales of ghosts, ghouls, and things that go bump in the night took over.

You may now be thinking that I must have felt more at home, but you would be mistaken. Sitting there, listening intently to all that was being said, only made me draw more into my shell. I think I felt more isolated because it was becoming obvious that these people, although ready to accept that strange things did indeed occur, had met with very limited experiences; mine had begun to take over my life.

I said nothing at all, willing the proceedings to end. Then, without preamble, during a lull in the conversation, Paul Denham said: "We haven't heard anything yet from the young lady sitting next to John. Rosemary, isn't it? Tell us about your experiences."

I felt my face go red, burning red. And I knew in that moment what a cornered animal feels like. The feeling of panic hit me for the second time that night, and I replied as steadily as I could.

"I have never had any experience of the paranormal. I don't see things, I don't feel things, and I don't ever sense anything."

Irene Denham spoke up. "I don't believe you," she said. "I think you have had many strange things happen to you which you don't understand. My husband, Paul, is a healer, and has been in the spiritualist movement for over thirty years. If you could just open up to us, maybe we could help you."

My mind raced briefly over the things she had said. Healers? Spiritualists? Was I hearing right? Christ was a healer. Did she mean that her husband was like Christ? But before I could assess any of this, Paul spoke again.

"The only way we can help you, Rosemary, is if you let us. And you could start by talking to us."

"If I talk to you, if I tell you about the weird things which have been going on around me," I heard myself saying aloud, "you will surely think I'm nuts."

"We won't think you're mad at all," he said very gently and sincerely. "I think it's time you told someone. Tell me."

If you have ever shaken a champagne bottle before popping the cork, you will know just how I felt. Everything just spurted out uncontrollably but explicitly as I began to describe all the peculiar events that had been taking place. You could have heard a pin drop. Faces of strangers looking at me—not laughing, as I thought they might, but appearing interested, curious.

I found myself talking of my experiences as a child when in the night the faces would come and the whisperings would begin. I told of how many times in my life I had been transported, as if by magic, to a different time or place in the universe, to be with people I didn't know yet felt comfortable with . . . until I had to explain it to myself later. I told of my visions and of how I would sometimes sit in a room . . . and see not the room, but another place entirely.

The more I talked, the more I found I had to say, and then I saw it, quite naturally and quite clearly. It was just like being in a cinema when the lights grow dim and the people all around you fade into the background. Then the screen lights up, showing the picture bright and clear and larger than life, so all-consuming that it pulls you through the void which separates the real from the unreal, allowing you to become part of the scene being unfolded before you.

Without realizing what was happening I had gone into a "trance state," and I was now to experience something that would change my life forever.

I saw before me an ocean, a large, cold, and uninviting sea, and approaching from the right-hand side came an enormous gray battleship. Very slowly it sailed toward me, and as it came into view I became aware of a lady standing on the deck. The dress she wore was long and gray, taken in at the waist. It seemed very plain except for a badge, about an inch round, which was sewn onto the bodice. On her head was a bonnet, which apart from the color, also gray, appeared similar to those worn by the ladies of the Salvation Army today.

I was just about to speak to her when I realized, with a shock, that this lady had no face. I know this sounds incredible, but where her features should have been, there were none. No eyes, no nose, no mouth . . . just a blank mask.

As I watched, her arms reached out to me beseechingly, and I heard her voice, as if from nowhere, crying out for help.

Even as this was happening, the ship began to tilt and the bow plunged down into the sea. The ship was sinking, and the lady in gray was drowning. Again she reached out to me and I heard her voice begging me, pleading to me for help.

I stood and watched and did nothing. I could do nothing!

Just as I thought it was all over, the whole thing started again, as though someone were rerunning a film. Three times the scene was enacted before me, and each time the cries for help, sounding so desperate, reached my ears. I knew with absolute certainty that she would be lost unless I did something.

But what could I do?

So helpless did I feel, her pleas so heartrending, that I burst into tears.

As quickly as it had started, it stopped. Back through the void I came, back to the "real world," only to discover, to my horror, the same group of strangers staring at me—now not with interest or curiosity, but, it seemed to me, as if I were an alien from outer space.

How long it had lasted I didn't know, and apparently, although I had been completely unaware of it, I had been recounting everything I had seen and heard. With tears still streaming down my face and my blouse soaked, I looked at their faces. Some were registering fright, others pure astonishment, Jean's among them. One or two showed sheer disbelief. I didn't blame them, any of them. I knew I was crazy, and now so did they. But it had all been so real!

Suddenly one of the group, a man in his early fifties, jumped up and started shouting at me, accusing me of "being in with the Denhams" and stating that the whole thing had been fixed. He shouted that the entire episode had been prearranged.

What whole thing? What was he talking about? I couldn't understand him at the time because I didn't realize the impact of what had happened or the effect it had had on everyone else. Grabbing his wife, who had been sitting dumbfounded, as by now were the rest of the assembly, he stalked out of the house.

It had obviously been a startling experience for all of us,

and all I could do was apologize. I have never been the sort of person to show my feelings in public, let alone cry, no matter how I felt. But here I had sat, having cried broken-heartedly and without restraint, not even realizing I was doing it. It was a humiliation for me, and I felt very embarrassed. Someone brought me a cup of tea, and I was told that I mustn't worry, that no one thought I was crazy.

Everyone was so kind to me, treating me like a small lost child, but all I could think about was the "lady in gray." It had been one of the most moving experiences of my life.

Jean, the friend who had brought me to this house, normally a forthright and outspoken person, was very subdued, not knowing what to make of things. So when I asked her again, "Please take me home," it was for her a tremendous relief.

Paul Denham insisted on walking us out to the car, and as we approached it he took hold of my arm, and looking directly into my eyes, he said: "You are not crazy, and one day soon you will realize that you are one of the sanest people on this earth."

Later, many days later, he was to say these words to me: "You are the greatest undeveloped medium my wife and I have ever met."

I was also to discover later, when working with Paul and Irene, that the events that had taken place on that summer night had been, in fact, my first experience with other people present, of working as a medium in trance.

And the "lady in gray?" I was to realize much later, as my gift became more developed, as I learned more, that she was a symbol for all those in the spirit world who desperately cry out for help. For those who look for someone who can help them to gain access to their loved ones, those who are still on "this side" of life, in order to reassure them of their existence in the afterlife.

With Paul's words ringing in my ears, I climbed quickly into the car. Jean had already started the motor, as much in a hurry now to be off as I, and we made a hasty retreat.

By this time I was beginning to believe that not only was I crackers, but that everyone else in that house must be, too. My friend could hardly wait to get rid of me, and when we reached my house I had barely gotten out of the car before she zoomed off into the night.

Going straight to bed, I lay for a long time thinking things through, the memory of the lady in gray coming back to me again and again. Try as I might, I could not understand what had happened or why, and eventually, some hours later in the early morning, I drifted off to sleep.

The
Healer
Man

Somewhere a phone was ringing, and in my sleepy haze I wondered why no one was answering it. Then, slowly, consciousness dawned. I realized that of course no one else was there, and my hand reached out and groped for that infernal machine I knew was somewhere on the floor by the bed. Who on earth could be ringing at this time in the morning? I peered at the clock through half-closed eyes and saw that it was nine-thirty A.M.—then suddenly I was wide awake, remembering the events of the night before. The lady in gray!

I picked up the receiver, and a voice said: "This is Irene Denham here, and I'm phoning to see if it would be possible for my husband, Paul, and me to come and talk to you."

Immediately I was on my guard and, very warily, asked: "Why?"

She explained that she and her husband were very interested in me, and after what had taken place the night before, perhaps they could help me.

This was beginning to sound more and more spooky, and my answer was guarded.

"I really don't feel very interested in what has happened," I said. "As far as I am concerned, spiritualism is something which should be left strictly alone."

Now you have to remember that I knew very little about spiritualism. My ideas were primitive, confined to things like people holding hands round a table, dark rooms, and hushed voices whispering, "Is there anybody there?"

From the age of three I had attended Sunday school, not because my mother believed that religious instruction was important, but because it was a way of getting us out from under her feet for an hour or so. The church I went to was a small building that stood on what seemed (to me as a child) to be a hill at the top of the road where we lived. Saffron Lane was a busy road situated on the outskirts of the city of Leicester, but on Sundays there would be little traffic, and my mother would usher us out the garden gate and see us off up the road. Many was the time in my early childhood that I would go with sore legs or a sore bottom and tears raining down my cheeks because I would kick up about not wanting to go.

Since I was always "the difficult one," my mother must have been pleased to "see the back of me," as she used to put it, on many occasions.

My church, as I still like to think of it, is called the Church of Christ, and although I rarely visit Leicester these days, when I do and I drive past that small Baptist church and see the wall that I used to sit on with my pals, I feel a pull at my heartstrings. As a teenager, whenever I felt sad or alone, I would sit on that little wall and talk to God.

The congregation was large, and the people I met at

church and grew up with were responsible for my religious upbringing. I had wonderful teachers, and the love and warmth I received from them at a time in my life when I felt none at home, I can still feel today. When I was fifteen years old I committed myself to living my life in the way that I felt Christ had shown through His teachings, so I was baptized. Some of you might think that at fifteen a young girl may not know her own mind, but I knew then, as I know now, that my life belonged to God and that I could trust Him to decide my fate in all things.

Now here I was, nearly twenty years later, aged thirty-five, listening to a woman I had met only the night before, talking about spirits and mediums. Even though I had said I wasn't interested, she hadn't been put off by my attitude at all. I imagine she had come up against it before.

Again she pressed home the point that I needed someone to talk to about the strange things that had been happening to me, someone who would understand and be able to help. Eventually, after a lot of persuasion, I was talked into going to her house for tea later that day. But the apprehension stayed with me.

Driving back to that place took an awful lot of courage for me, as I didn't know what I was letting myself in for, but my instincts told me that once I had entered the Denhams' house again, my life would change completely. The problem was that I didn't know how, or in what way, or even if I wanted it to. Only my faith in God sustained me and gave me the courage to step over the threshold and into a new world.

Tea was a small affair, just the Denhams, two dogs, a cat, and me. At first they explained that they were new to the area and had been trying, quite successfully, it seemed, to organize a group of people, who met every Friday evening, to discuss the paranormal. I have since learned that "paranormal" covers an enormous scope, including alternative healing. Irene, as I was asked to call her, had managed to persuade people, like John the tarot card reader from the night before, to come to the group and give a talk on their given subject.

She informed me that for next Friday's meeting they were expecting a practicing healer from Doncaster, South Yorkshire, in the north of England. It seemed quite natural that the conversation should then turn toward spiritualism, and before I knew it I was asking questions, and more questions. My curiosity was overcoming my fear, and my thirst for knowledge had begun.

So many things were said on that fateful Saturday afternoon, and so many fears were washed away. My mind was by no means clear, but because I had finally been able to talk to people who really seemed able to understand and who explained some of my experiences, the cobwebs began to blow away.

It was decided that every Wednesday evening Paul, Irene, and I would meet so that I could develop my psychic abilities.

I had approached this suggestion with extreme caution and was not at all sure that I wanted to become more involved in that way. Talking about the paranormal and reading about it can be fascinating, but to put yourself directly in the firing line, to experience firsthand on a one-to-one basis communication with "ghosts" or "dead people," is definitely something else again. The longer I spoke with Paul and Irene, the more my confidence in them grew. It was confidence in myself that was lacking. However, my appetite had been whetted, and I felt that I must give it a try.

The following Wednesday evening at seven-thirty I arrived once more at the little white cottage in the middle of nowhere. This was to become a familiar pattern over the next few months, and the cottage was to become, for a time, almost my second home.

Nothing much happened at this, my first attempt at developing my gift. First Paul said a prayer, asking God for His help, guidance, and protection. This call for protection was all-important to me, and I found it very comforting. Nevertheless my own silent prayer, I remember, was a fervent request to God for protection against all evil. Especially, I thought, oh yes, especially, against any little demons that might be lurking unseen in any of the dark corners of that small, quiet room where the three of us sat.

My faith in God, and in His ability to know better than I did about what was good and what represented evil, enabled me that night to sit with confidence. Shaky confidence, I must add, as my nerves were taut and I was very much on edge.

I prayed hard that night, and I have prayed hard ever since, for guidance and the strength to do God's will.

There are many people who refer to mediums as the devil's instruments and accuse us of doing the devil's work. These same people also speak of the love of Christ and of the love we must have for our fellow man. The love of God is something that all so-called religious people talk freely about.

Now, as I am not acquainted with the devil—in fact, not even on speaking terms with him (or her)—it would be wrong of me to try to describe what kind of work he might have in mind, either for me or for any other medium.

Perhaps because of my early involvement with the church, I have grown up with God, and because there has always been a regular and sincere form of communication between us, a strong bond has been formed. Because my love for Him is strong and my earnest desire is to do His will, the only work that I have done, or will ever do, is in God's name.

There are many religions in this world, preaching many things, but the one message they all share is that God is love. Put your faith and trust in God, they say, and He will protect you always. That is exactly what I have done.

It is my belief that no one religion has got it absolutely right, not even spiritualism. I am not qualified to understand God's intentions, nor do I believe that there is anyone else on this earth who does. All any of us can do, and all, I'm sure, that He expects of us, is right thinking, in our own way, as individuals. To think loving thoughts, and to have a caring attitude toward our fellows, and to try to live in peace and harmony with each other.

My firm belief is that this is what God's requirements of us are, and if we ask His help, no matter what religious label we have chosen, He will look into our hearts and make His judgment there.

All these thoughts, and more, had gone through my mind after my first talk with Paul and Irene, and as we sat that first Wednesday evening I found comfort in the knowledge that Paul himself had been a practicing healer for over thirty years. He had trained as a young man, had met many mediums and healers, and had sat in many development groups. Sometimes he would tell me of his experiences, of the strange, often incredible occurrences he had witnessed over the years. How he had seen apports—gifts from the spirit world, such as flowers or small trinkets—appear, as if by magic, before his eyes. How he had played with ecto-plasm—a kind of fluid that emanates from a trance medium—held it in his hands, seen mediums change their physical appearance, heard their voices change dramatically.

Never have I met anyone as caring and gentle as Paul Denham. Although he has been involved with spiritualism for three decades, I have never heard him shout about it or push his beliefs onto anyone else. His quiet manner belies his strength of character and purpose, and his attitude to-ward others is one of gentle sincerity. His gift of healing is most obvious, I think, when he deals with animals, who take to him immediately. Even the most restless of them settle down under his loving hands. Animals get sick, too, and Paul has a special talent when it comes to giving healing to them.

As we sat quietly, waiting, for what I wasn't sure, I could feel Paul's presence, warm and reassuring. And while I lis-tened in that quiet room to the muffled ticking of the clock, my eyes began to close and I started to feel quite drowsy. Then, very slowly, I felt as if I were being drawn down into what I can only describe as a large black pit. At first it seemed so natural, and I was so relaxed, that by this time it didn't worry me. I seemed to be moving, floating, down, down, down. My body was stationary, but "I"—my mind—my senses—my being—had begun a "journey." It felt com-fortable and easy, not at all a new experience. I had been on "journeys" like this before, never with anyone present, and because I had assumed that this was part of my "craziness," I had been afraid and had always at some point struggled for control of my mind.

As I traveled, in a kind of dreamlike state, farther and farther into this dark space, my limbs became heavy and my whole body became a dead weight. Then, in an instant, and just in time, I realized what was happening. I was about to lose control of my conscious thoughts, to enter a trance state. My mind screamed out, *No!* and I jerked myself back forcibly from the brink of unconsciousness. Within seconds I was wide awake, and from then on I stayed alert, making sure that I didn't become drowsy again.

Strangely enough, I was not even one little bit afraid, not in the way I had been before. I had, with effort, been able to pull myself back from the void, to stop myself from being carried away. I had known instinctively that it was important to stay as much in control as I could. In fact, it was imperative. And all these years later, I still feel the same.

On many occasions since I have become involved with the "paranormal," as it is called, I have witnessed mediums working in "trance," and I always ask the same questions: Is it real? Has that person really been taken over by some spirit entity who is speaking through them, or is the trance self-induced? Unfortunately, most of the time I have had to come up with the all-too-usual answer: that the "medium," consciously or otherwise, is faking! There are many reasons why someone might fake a trance state. Some people so desperately want to be mediums, they may have a need not only to be able to communicate with the spirit world, but to be seen by others to have this ability. Consciously or subconsciously they act the part, often fooling themselves more than others because they think that it looks good. After all, communicating through trance is what real mediums are said to do. I myself through the years have had countless experiences of trance work, some of which I will recount later in this story, but at the beginning of my development it was impossible for me to tell the fake trance from the real, both with myself and with other people. So the only way I felt I could make sure that I wasn't being fooled, or that I wasn't fooling myself, was to remain critical and in control of all situations.

As I drove home later that evening it occurred to me that my lack of fear was really quite amazing, and I also realized how much at home I had felt. Not so much at the Denhams' house, but with the idea of making contact with those in spirit. But for what reason I did not yet know.

Climbing into bed that night, I did what I always do: I prayed silently, asking God for His help and guidance. But this time I put in a special request. Please, I said, give me a sign, let me know if what I am doing is right and if it is what You want.

I didn't expect my answer to come quite so soon, or in the way that it came, but as soon as I laid my head on the pillow and closed my eyes, His response was immediate and clear.

I knew instinctively who they were. I heard them quite distinctly, and in total harmony, I heard them singing. Angels—singing!

Sitting bolt upright, I looked around the room, peering into the corners. Goodness knows what I expected to see, but there was no one there, of course. Still the singing continued, and it really did sound just as you might imagine angels would sound: clear and sweet, their voices holding an ethereal quality.

And just what, you might ask, were they singing . . . these angels?

Well, I'll tell you—they were singing that well-known psalm, the Twenty-third.

The Lord is my shepherd, I shall not want.
He makes me down to lie,
In pastures green, He leadeth me,
The quiet waters by.

I lay back down again and listened, as over and over those words were sung. Then, smiling my thanks and like a baby being sung a lullaby, I went to sleep.

Two weeks later I went with Paul on my first visit to a spiritualist church, in the city of Doncaster, in South Yorkshire. I was a little apprehensive, as I had no idea what to expect. A spiritualist church is run on similar lines to most orthodox churches, the difference being that in place of a minister they would have a speaker, and usually but not always a medium, to conduct the service. After hymns are sung, a short talk is given, the topic concerning life after death, what that may mean to us all, how it can affect our daily lives, and so forth. Prayers are said, and then, if a medium is present, the last twenty to thirty minutes of the service will entail the medium making communication with the spirit world and the giving of messages from those in spirit, via the medium, to members of the congregation. The service always ends with the congregation joining together in prayer that acknowledges the presence of the spirit world and its influence upon us.

As we sat, waiting for the service to begin, Paul looked through the little hymn book we had been given. The hymns we were to sing that night were listed on the wall, and Paul was looking to see what they were.

Opening the book to the first hymn listed, he grinned, nudged me, and handed it to me. The words seemed to leap up from the page and bounce in front of me, and I laughed out loud as I read the written message.

"The Lord is my shepherd."

For the next few years, each time I questioned or doubted myself and the work I had begun to do, I would hear those voices, those angels singing, and always the same hymn. The Twenty-third Psalm.

The following Friday I again made my way to the Denhams' house, and this time I was quite looking forward to the evening. Although I was a little nervous about seeing all those people who had witnessed my odd behavior during the previous meeting, my curiosity was now fully aroused.

As I had no baby-sitter that night, I had brought my daughter, Samantha, with me. Paul and Irene had made up the beds in the spare room, and I had agreed to stay overnight. Even though it was only a fifteen-minute drive from the Denhams' house to my own, I had been pleased to accept the offer to stay, as I expected Samantha, who was just eleven years old, to fall asleep during the visit and didn't like the idea of disturbing her.

This evening's speaker was a gentleman who for the last five years had been president of the spiritualist church in Doncaster, and he had been a practicing healer for several years. He was short and stockily built, in his mid-thirties. He spoke with a northern accent and gave a solid and down-to-earth appearance.

Paul and Irene had invited him to give a talk on healing, which turned out to be fascinating. He explained that, as a healer, he did what is known as "laying on his hands," much as Christ had done. After placing his hands on his patient's shoulders, or simply holding his patient's hands in his, he would offer up a silent prayer to God and to the universe for help to still the spirit of his patient, for healing to be given, by God, to the spirit self, so that the patient would discover an inner peace, an inner calm, enabling him to deal better with his physical or mental ailment. Although there are occasions when healing is obvious and instantaneous, often for the onlooker there would be nothing to see, no outer evidence that anything unusual had taken place. No drama, no great and visible cure, but a quiet and gentle way of healing that only the healer and the patient would be aware of. He further explained that it was his belief that only when the spirit self had been calmed, quieted, through healing, only then could healing of the physical body take place. He was a humorous speaker, and as I knew nothing at all then about this subject, I was spellbound. Afterward, while we sat with coffee and biscuits, many of the group asked questions about healing and how it felt to experience healing.

We were all obviously so interested that he offered to give each of us, in turn, a minute or two of healing in what he called a group session. Even though I was intrigued by this, I wasn't too happy about being directly involved, and I was very wary of diving headfirst into something I might not be able to handle. But I had no choice, as Irene, suspecting I might bolt, grabbed my hand, insisting that a little bit of healing was just what I needed.

The first thing we all had to do was join hands while the speaker said a prayer, asking for healing to be given. Then he stood in front of each of us and, one by one, took hold of our hands, and, standing quite still, asked God again for us to be given healing.

He had begun with the lady who was sitting next to me, and as he went slowly around the room I was able to see, quite well, all that he was doing.

No mumbo-jumbo, no peculiar chanting or strange rituals. Just an ordinary man, giving his love to each and every one of us in turn.

Carefully I watched people's faces, trying to assess their thoughts; and without exception everyone seemed pleased, relaxed, and happy with their experience. The atmosphere in the room was so peaceful, and as my turn came and the speaker reached out his hands to me I had no qualms at all. Placing my hands in his seemed the most natural thing to do, so I was completely unprepared for what happened next.

As he held my hands I began to shake. Slowly at first, and then, as if I had grabbed hold of a jackhammer, strange and strong vibrations began to run right through my whole body.

I sat, paralyzed, unable to move, unable to do or say anything, as the vibrations in my body grew in intensity until they reached my head. My mouth was filled with pins and needles, my teeth and gums shook violently, and my face was a ball of red hot fire.

Still the speaker held on to my hands, although it must have been difficult, as I was compelled then, by this phenomenal force, out of my chair. I stood, feeling as though I had been lifted bodily off the floor, still shaking furiously.

Terrified at what was happening, I was completely unaware that everyone else in the room had stood up, dazedly watching our two figures, mine and the healer's, convulsing uncontrollably in the middle of the room.

Somewhere inside of me I was striving for control of this thing, this terrible force, which was trying to consume my very being. Eventually, and with great effort, I let rip a yell, so fearsome that it must have sounded like an Indian war cry, and it was as if a spell had been broken.

Suddenly I was myself again, the pins and needles gone and the vibrations stopped. I felt like a limp and empty shell. Then my legs buckled, and I collapsed back onto the chair, feeling utterly exhausted. I could not stop the tears that began to rain down my face.

The speaker put his arm around me, and Irene, fussing over me like a mother hen, uttered an explanation to everyone that I had been under great stress lately and that my nerves had just snapped.

Someone brought me a cup of tea, and as I sat there, grateful for the hot liquid burning down my throat, I remember thinking, Never again. Never again will I let anyone like him, anyone "psychic," touch me.

As I looked around the room I felt once again ashamed of myself, so foolish, and I was convinced that the whole group would think of me as some sort of exhibitionist.

They'll definitely think I'm crackers now, I thought. And they are right. I really am cracking up.

Samantha, blissfully asleep in the guest room, was my excuse now for leaving the group. I climbed the stairs, grateful to be away from all those people, and went into the room where Samantha lay. Everything here was quiet except for the sound of gentle breathing as my child slept, oblivious of all around her. Sitting carefully on the bed, I thought hard about all that had happened only a few minutes before.

The speaker had felt what I had felt, of that I was sure. But why? Why had it happened, and how? I was no longer frightened, simply puzzled by the whole thing.

I stayed in the comfort of that peaceful room, with Samantha, for nearly an hour, until I heard the guests below leaving, calling good night. Only when I thought that everyone had gone did I make my way down the stairs, wondering what the Denhams' reaction would be to my ridiculous behavior.

Quietly I closed the bedroom door and started across the landing, when for the second time that night I almost leapt out of my skin with fright. Out of the shadows loomed the figure of a man, and only just in time, before I started to scream out, I recognized the man who had come to give the group a talk—the healer man.

He explained quickly that he had been waiting for me because he realized how frightened I had been.

"Come and talk to me," he said. "I would like to explain to you what happened, and why."

We went back to the sitting room, where Paul and Irene had also been waiting.

I was forced to smile, because the first thing the healer man said was, "After I have explained some things to you, it's likely that you'll think I'm crazy." (Do those words sound familiar?)

He continued, telling me that he also had experienced the vibrations, and he described exactly everything that he had felt.

I knew that he was telling the truth because only someone who had experienced those weird sensations could possibly know, and describe, the things that he knew. Then, looking hard at me, he said:

"You are not going to believe what I am going to say next, but you will remember, and when the time is right, full understanding will be yours.

"You are a medium, a natural medium, and you have a guide, a very strong and powerful spiritual guide, who, one day soon, will make himself known to you. This spirit guide will be your mentor, your teacher in all things. I can't tell you who it is, I don't know him. But I can tell you this, he is one of the strongest forces I have ever come across in all the years that I have been involved in spiritualism."

He then went on to tell me a little more about spirit guides and told me that his guide, a Native American chief called Red Feather, was a healing guide who helped many healers in their spiritual work.

"What has happened here tonight," he continued, "is that my guide, Red Feather, has met and acknowledged your guide. When we held hands our guides, yours and mine, joined forces, and the tremendous surge of energy which we then felt was enough, literally, to knock us both off our feet."

This was the first time I had heard mention of spirit guides, and strangely I was willing to accept the possibility of such things. But to expect me to believe in the existence of a ghostly Indian chief . . . ? Oh, no! That really sounded too farfetched and impossible, and I told him so.

"You're right," I said, "I don't believe you, and I definitely think that you are crazy."

The healer man laughed at this, and with a knowing smile, which I found very disconcerting, he took his leave. His parting shot to me, as he walked out of the door, was this: "You think that I'm crazy, and you also doubt your own sanity, but very soon now you will be shown just how sane we both are. Remember," he said, "you are on the threshold of a new life. Don't be afraid!"

The following Wednesday evening came around quickly—too quickly, in fact, for I had not yet made up my mind whether or not to continue with Irene and Paul in what they had called my psychic development. The three of us had had many discussions over the two weeks we had been working together. Paul's instincts had told him that my development was important, but he was unsure about the reasons. We had no goal in mind, just a need to explore. Even though I had known them only a short time, my instincts told me that they genuinely wanted to help me, and I trusted them. But the doubts about myself persisted.

Sitting at home, weighing the pros and cons of the matter, had only seemed to confuse me more, so finally I decided to give it one more try—just one!

I arrived at the Denhams' house late and a little bit flustered, so I didn't notice, as I pulled into their drive, that there was another car parked, unfamiliar to me.

Irene was waiting for me at the door and showed me through to the kitchen, where, hardly giving myself time to get off my coat, I began to explain my feelings.

"I'm not sure," I began. "I just don't know whether I am able to handle all of this psychic stuff."

Almost as if reading my mind, Irene replied, "I'll tell you what we'll do. Let's just give it one more try, shall we? And if you still feel unsure, then we'll stop until you're ready to try again. How's that?"

With a sigh of relief, I nodded, and as Irene put the kettle on to make tea, I made my way into the sitting room— only to find myself confronted by another obstacle.

"Hello," said a voice as I walked into the room, and I found myself, once again, face-to-face with the man I had met the previous Friday evening—the healer man, this stranger who had spoken so easily of Indians and spirit guides. As I sat down I wondered how soon I could possibly leave without seeming impolite to my hosts, and I was sure that the healer man could sense my discomfort.

Explaining that he had been asked by the Denhams if he would like to join our little Wednesday group, he smiled at me and said he hoped that I wouldn't mind, knowing full well that I did. He went on to tell me how fascinated he had been that last Friday, as he, too, had felt the force of the vibrations, and how this had been a new experience for him.

None of this chitchat made me feel any easier, and as I looked at him across the room, I thought gloomily that I should never have come. He rambled on for a bit longer but I wasn't really listening much, until suddenly he said something that made the hairs on the back of my neck bristle. If any of you have ever seen a dog's hackles rise up, then you'll know just what I mean. Staring hard at him, dumbfounded by what I'd just heard, I gasped and managed to croak out:

"What was that? What did you say?"

Realizing instantly that he had startled me, he said, "Oh, Rosemary, I'm so sorry, I didn't mean to frighten or upset you in any way, but you see, I'm afraid I just had to tell you." And then he repeated once more:

"There is a gentleman from the spirit world, Rosemary, standing just behind you, wearing a soldier's uniform, with sergeant's stripes. He is telling me that he was an army man all his life, and he has given me his name—William Edward."

The hairs on the back of my neck were now standing bolt upright, and a prickling heat was searing its way through my whole body, and I sat there, unable to move or speak, the shock of what I had just heard was so great.

No one, not one single soul, neither my friends nor my neighbors in the north of England, could have supplied this man with the information he had just given me. How, I thought, after only one previous meeting, could this near stranger describe to me so accurately a man who had been "dead" for over four years?

And the name, William Edward, it was so close, too close to dismiss the obvious, the only plausible explanation—the man, the army sergeant, must indeed have been standing, like a ghost, behind me. And only he could have told the healer man his name, not William Edward, but William Edwards—my father!

My dazed state didn't seem to disturb the healer man at all. He continued, giving me information about the way my father had died and about the kind of person he was. He told me that my father had had a massive heart attack, dying instantly. Further, he proceeded to describe my father's character, particularly in relation to his army career, saying that he was a stubborn and proud man, intolerant of imperfection both in others and himself. This information was correct in every detail.

I knew then, as I have always believed, that life after death was a fact, and many times since my father's passing I had felt him with me. So it wasn't the shock of being told that he was there beside me that had shaken me as much as the fact that someone else could see, as I had done, a person who was supposed to be dead.

After the initial shock of all of this, I began to feel a kind of excitement bubbling deep inside of me. And then a rapturous joy spread slowly over me as realization dawned.

A stranger had given me absolute evidence, without question, of my father's survival after death and of his ability to communicate beyond the grave.

With this knowledge that I had just acquired came hope, not just for myself, but for the whole of humanity. And I was also given, in that moment, peace, an inner peace, and I knew with certainty that everything I had ever experienced in my life had a purpose.

All the heartaches and fears, all the strange and unexplainable happenings of the last thirty-four years, the weird sights and sounds that had led me to believe that I was indeed losing my mind, suddenly made sense. I knew, once and for all, that I was sane, that my mind was perfectly balanced, and I realized that not only did the healer man have the gift of "sight," but that I too shared that gift.

So many people had visited me since my childhood, people from the spirit world, trying to help me and to make me aware of the precious gift I had been born with. Yet it took a stranger, someone with this same gift, to make me see that what I had been doing since I was a child, seeing and hearing "ghosts," was perfectly natural, and not frightening at all.

Now I heard the healer man saying, "Come here, come and sit next to me and hold my hand and I will try, if I can, to talk some more with the army sergeant, who, by the way, has informed me that he has waited for four years to talk to you. Four years for him to find someone with whom he could communicate, someone who could see and hear him."

Eagerly now, I did as he asked and was given many messages from my father for all of the family. But even though everything the healer man said was accurate, my suspicious mind was telling me to be careful. So I sat with my head well down, taking care not to look at him, while I thought, Don't look at him, don't let him read your face. I didn't want to give this man any indication that I knew what he was talking about or a way to gauge anything from my reactions. In other words, I didn't want to give anything away.

I realize now that this reaction was a sort of protection

against the possibility of mind reading, and quite a few of my own clients have, at first, the same reaction to me.

When people come to see me privately for a sitting and avert their eyes, or keep their heads down, I always smile and remember my own first encounter with spirit through a third person.

But back to the healer man—it was only when he gave me the name of Judith that I opened up a little, and I told him that she was my sister. He described her, tall, blond, and blue eyed, and talked of her divorce and how difficult her life had been. He also mentioned that she had two children, a boy and a girl, and he talked a little of them, too. It was amazing, all of it; everything he said was just so incredible, but true.

The last message, however, was one that at the time didn't make much sense.

"I am being shown a ring," he said, "a large oval-shaped ruby, surrounded by diamonds, in a setting which is so beautiful. The diamonds themselves must be worth a fortune, and the ruby is the most wonderful color, deep red, clear and pure, not a flaw in it, a perfect stone."

I began rubbing my hands together; after all, everything else he had said had been right, so perhaps I was going to meet a millionaire who would shower me with diamonds and rubies. Although greed and avarice are not usually part of my nature, I must admit that my eyes did sparkle just a little at the prospect of all this.

But when the healer man explained the full meaning of this message, I realized that wealth comes in many forms.

The ring, the beautiful ruby, was a symbol of clairvoyance, as the color red indicates, as pure and clear as possible.

The setting of diamonds is symbolic of the beauty and energy that always surrounds me when I'm working.

I was being shown something precious, a thing of beauty that I must cherish, so rare and so special. An indication of the mediumship that was to come.

This precious gift from God, which I had been blessed with since I was a child, was going to be developed, brought out, so that all of those who wished could share with me the wondrous knowledge of spirit.

While I had been sitting, engrossed with the healer man, in communication with my father, I had completely forgotten the reason I had gone to visit Paul and Irene that evening. But now my sitting was drawn to a close, and the Denhams appeared in the doorway to ask if we were ready to begin the "circle."

They both looked very pleased with themselves, and I realized that they had deliberately kept out of the way but had been listening in the kitchen to all that had been said.

My impromptu sitting had, it would appear, benefited all of us, so as we formed a circle and held hands, and as Paul opened our meeting with a protective prayer, a feeling of calm and peace enveloped us all. Until, that is, the man who had just given me such fantastic evidence stood up and without preamble started playacting in front of my very eyes. As I sat in semidarkness I watched the healer man "pretend" to be an Indian chief. It was so ludicrous that I almost laughed out loud. Yet at the same time my mind was telling me that the man standing before me was good. There was no way he could have done what he had ten minutes before if he wasn't real. So why start pretending now?

Part of me wanted to believe him, and part of me, the

sensible part, simply couldn't accept Indian chiefs as anything other than, at best, part of an overactive imagination.

After I had met this man the first time, and he had mentioned guides, I had gone away and read up a little on the subject of spirit guides. The one thing that struck me more than anything else was that so many of these guides seemed to be American Indians. So farfetched did this seem to me at the time that I dismissed it all as rubbish.

I sat mulling over all of this, not really listening anymore to what was being said. Why, I thought, do they always have to be American Indians? If mediums do have spirit guides, then why can't they be something more credible, less exotic?

Eventually, the "playacting" over, we closed the circle and the healer man asked me what I had thought of his guide, Red Feather.

Although I felt very uncomfortable, as I found it difficult to criticize this man because of my earlier experience with him, I still felt bound to tell the truth. I told him that it was impossible for me to believe there were Indian chiefs with nothing better to do than "float" around, waiting for someone to guide.

"If ever I have a guide, which I doubt," I said, "and if I ever get to the stage where I accept that such things do exist, I can tell you one thing, it is certainly not going to be an Indian chief!"

The healer man smiled that infuriating smile—a smile I have since come to know and to understand—and he said, "Well, Rosemary, stranger things have happened, and perhaps one day I will be able to watch while you eat your words."

Many months passed before I did just that. During that

time, each Wednesday evening, our small group gathered to witness my startling progress.

The man who guided my development during this period, the healer man, was responsible for helping me to go carefully and to choose the right path. He was a constant source of information and wisdom, and he helped me at all times to find the strength within me that I needed to stay on that path.

He showed me that the answers to my questions were within me, and although he laughed at me often, over many things, he never ridiculed me. A better friend I could not have wished for than this gentle healer man, and I will be grateful to him always.

Oh, yes, I nearly forgot to tell you—his name is Mick McGuire!

PART II

Grey
Eagle

The
Eagle

It was Irene who first made the suggestion. "Give up your job," she said, "and put an advertisement in the local paper. You could give psychic readings, charge £3.50 for half an hour. . . . You could do it."

I was living in the small town of Epworth in the north of England, working in a pub behind the bar, part-time, earning a small but much needed wage. It wouldn't have been too bad if it hadn't been for the unwanted attentions of the lecherous landlord. Working for him became more and more impossible, but I had no choice, or so it seemed—my eleven-year-old needed feeding.

Considering Irene's suggestion, I realized I would need only three sessions a week to match what I was earning at the pub. But what if I couldn't do it . . . what if no one came?

I would hear the voices, now much clearer, urging me to leave, give up the job; but what would I do, how would I cope? I needed the money. I had begun to tell a few people about my experiences, and I had told my sister what our father had said, through Mick McGuire, which she totally accepted.

So I made a pact. "All right," I said to those in the spirit world I knew were listening. "The first week I get three bookings I'll give up my job and work full-time for the spirit world." The following week I quit my job and chose my new name . . . Altea. That was in October 1981.

Bookings came in slowly over the next few months, but there were never fewer than three a week. At first I was terribly nervous, knowing the responsibility of what I was doing and aware of the great need of those in the spirit world to communicate with their loved ones. I worked hard, wanting to do my very best. Even though I seemed to be working in the dark, I was always aware that someone was helping me, although I didn't know who. . . .

Even as I write this chapter I contemplate the low probability of being believed, knowing how ridiculous it all seems. Although one of the main aims in my life is to help people to understand how normal and natural a medium's work is, I do seem to be saying just the opposite. What I am about to write I know will be seen as so ludicrous as to be totally unbelievable. I am also aware of the danger, more so after writing such seeming rubbish, of being thought by some to be a liar, a cheat, and a charlatan.

What I am about to relate lacks credence, I know. Yet it's true.

My first meeting with a spirit guide did not occur in dramatic and unusual circumstances, as I might have expected.

It was just a few weeks after I had begun my psychic development, November 1981, that I woke early one morning to find him standing by the bed, looking down at me. Although I was still half asleep, I knew he was no apparition, no specter in the night. Nor was he a figment of my imagination.

It felt natural for me to acknowledge him, and I smiled a sleepy hello.

He bowed graciously, looking completely at ease, and I knew that subconsciously I had been waiting for this moment to arrive.

I didn't ask his name, and he never gave it, but I nicknamed him my dancing Scotsman.

He wore a bright-colored kilt and a jacket, with a sword belt strapped across his shoulder and a sporran laid over the kilt; on his head he wore a tam-o'-shanter. His shoes were soft and looked similar to those worn by ballet dancers, and his socks were the long woolen type.

And he danced. Every time he was pleased with something, or if he felt that I needed cheering up, which was quite often in those days, he would dance a little jig.

I didn't need to be told that he was a spirit guide, or helper. I knew instinctively that he was, and I felt tremendously reassured just having him around.

I began to expect him to be there when I needed help of any kind, and every morning when I woke up he would be the first person I would see.

It was great to have someone special—a friend, a teacher—and without realizing it, I became quite reliant on the fact that he was always there when I needed him. Basically, I took him for granted.

A silly thing to do.

Having read quite a bit by this time about spirit guides,

books like *Forty Years a Medium* written by Estelle Roberts, I knew that all of us have someone in the spirit world who watches us and watches over us. For most people this "guide," or "guardian angel," is someone connected to the family, a relative or close friend, often someone we have had a special affinity with prior to his or her death. Occasionally this guide may be family connected but never talked about, so we may have to do some checking to discover his (or her) identity. I had just assumed that I had been allocated my dancing Scotsman, who was possibly some ancient ancestor, rather than an American Indian, and that from now on he would always be around to help with my work and personal life.

I was quite delighted with this choice of guide, as I have always felt a particular affinity with the Scottish people, and indeed with Scotland itself, and I loved to hear him when he spoke to me, his voice soft and lilting. My father, being half Welsh, half Scot, had always seemed to dismiss the Welsh side of the family and was very proud of his Scottish an-cestry. I suppose this is where my own feelings stemmed from.

Apart from this, I felt that a Scottish guide was much more acceptable in real terms than some possibly imagined, outlandish-seeming Indian chief with feathers in his hair and perhaps war paint on his face.

So I was content. My psychic development was unusual, I was told by Mick and Paul, in that everything I attempted to do, to learn, came easily. Instinctively I knew how to act and how to react. It was as if, suddenly, someone had switched on a light. I had been plugged in to some incredi-ble unseen energy source, and I knew just how to use it. My actions were totally spontaneous, and as I sat with my clients, making communication with their loved ones in the spirit world, I knew just what to do.

If my dancing Scotsman, always with me, wanted to communicate certain information to me quickly, the most efficient way was to show me certain pictures or symbols. He didn't have to explain these symbols, or signs, to me. I just knew instinctively (there's that word again) what they meant. It was a bit like learning the highway code, using road signs to indicate certain situations, such as a railway crossing, road construction ahead, and so on.

I cannot be specific about the symbols that we used, nor their meanings. I do not imply that these are secret signs, trade secrets, so to speak, but this is a language all of its own, foreign to most people. It is a language I still use, but it has become more complex, less simplistic, and totally unexplainable. And, like the old proverb, every picture tells a story, or, in this case, one picture is worth a thousand words.

My clientele began to grow, I continued with my development group, my clairvoyant and clairaudient abilities became stronger and therefore much clearer, and each Wednesday evening as Paul, Irene, Mick, and I met to continue my psychic development, my progress was, to say the least, startling.

All this time my dancing Scotsman was there helping, pushing, encouraging, and every morning I would wake to find him smiling down at me and ready to begin another day. I was happy. I drew closer to God, knowing that I was doing His work.

I can't remember exactly when it was that I began to be aware of yet another strong influence about me. It was a distinctly male influence, and at first I thought it was my father. But I soon dismissed this theory, as it didn't "feel" right. It is hard to explain to those who have never had a psychic experience the feeling of a "presence"—a sensing of a "spirit being" around you, sometimes close, almost breathing on you, sometimes from a distance, but real, very real.

It must have been in January 1982, just two or three months after meeting the Scotsman, and at first I put it down to mild curiosity on the part of someone in spirit, come to take a look at me and at what was going on.

It soon became apparent that whoever this was, he was more than just mildly curious. He was around far too often for that. But try as I might, I could not catch even a glimpse of this unknown intruder.

Even Mick was at a loss as to who he was, but smiling that knowing smile, which I had now come to recognize so well, he told me that I would just have to be patient and wait until "he," whoever "he" was, was ready to make himself known to me. "That is," he added, grinning wickedly, "if he ever does."

Then came the shock!

I woke up one morning and automatically turned to where my dancing Scotsman usually stood, but he was not there. I sat bolt upright and searched around the bedroom. He was nowhere in sight!

At first I panicked, wondering frantically if I had done or said anything that might have offended him. I couldn't think of anything, but I found it hard to dismiss the thought. Then common sense took over, and I realized how selfish I was being to expect him to be with me all the time.

He'll turn up when he's ready, I thought. Perhaps he's busy. I'm sure I'll see him later on.

Well, I waited. All that day I expected that he'd turn up, then the next day, and the next. But he didn't.

He had disappeared without any warning or explanation of any kind. My dancing Scotsman had deserted me. I felt lost, alone, and so let down. I thought this must be the end, the end of my work as a medium.

What I had yet to learn was that often, before new growth can take place, the gardener must till the land. And a good gardener always makes sure before he begins his work that the land is fertile. He would not plant a forest of young trees without first inspecting the ground to make sure that his trees would gain nourishment to enable them to grow tall and strong.

Two weeks passed, and it now seemed that my dancing Scotsman had gone forever. But the space in my life that he had occupied was slowly being filled. My mystery figure, the unknown spirit entity, was making his presence felt more and more. At first his "presence" had been spasmodic; now I "felt" him constantly, always there, drawing closer.

I began on Wednesday evenings to do more and more trance work.

While in trance, the medium chooses to vacate her physical body, for just a short time, leaving an empty shell or vessel, which a spirit entity may then use. Able to use the vocal cords, the spirit entity can then communicate "through" the medium to the other members of the group or circle, often telling of their own earthly life experiences and expounding their philosophical views and ideas about life, both on the earth plane and in the spirit world.

Basically there are three stages of trance: light, medium, and deep. The first state, light trance, is possibly the most interesting from the medium's point of view, as she (or he) is aware of everything that is happening, even though unable to interfere or stop it in any way.

In the first stage of trance, I was able to watch and listen with fascination as some unseen force seemed to manipulate "my" body as a puppeteer might operate his doll.

In the second stage of trance it is possible to be aware of some of the proceedings but not all. And in deep trance, the third stage, the medium is totally unaware of any action that takes place. This is why we always made sure we had on a tape recorder at all times during the evening. I have always hated to miss out on anything and found it infuriating to have to listen as, at the end of an evening of trance work, the rest of the group discussed with interest the events that had taken place. Only after listening to the tape could I join in and feel part of it all.

I was never very keen to go into trance. Not, as some of you might think, because I was scared, although on reflection I am surprised that I wasn't. But I was always concerned that my trance state was real, not my imagination working overtime. I certainly didn't want to fool anyone else. But more important, I didn't want to start fooling myself. I gained so much knowledge and insight through trance work, but at that stage in my development, going into trance seemed to me to be such an unnecessary thing to do.

So I always fought against it. Mick would sit with me and gently, patiently, talk me through my doubts until, once I was sufficiently relaxed, a trance state would take place.

During the short time that my dancing Scotsman had been with me, he had always been a gentle spirit guide, a quiet and sensitive teacher, always leading me by the hand in a calming and reassuring manner. This new entity, who, I began to suspect, was to take the Scotsman's place, was a different force altogether.

I didn't like not knowing who he was, and that made me

a little nervous. But I was more curious than afraid and began to look for little signs or clues as to who the mystery man was. And I sensed more and more that I would not have to wait much longer to find out.

The date was February 10, 1982. My daughter, Samantha, was not quite twelve years old. It was a Wednesday afternoon, and I was driving home from Doncaster along a straight country road, when it happened. I got my final clue. A huge bird seemed to come from out of the blue and flew straight across the hood of the car. My foot hit the brakes, and the car skidded to a halt, with me inside shaking like a leaf. I'd really thought I was going to hit the thing.

What was it? I thought. An eagle? No. It couldn't have been, we don't have eagles in this part of the country. But it was. As soon as I'd thought those words I knew that I was right.

I tried to picture it in my mind but only got the image of its underside, which had been grey.

I drove home, puzzling over what had happened, knowing that this incident definitely had something to do with the still unknown spirit entity who I now felt often, at my side. But what it meant I still didn't know. I just couldn't figure it out.

Samantha was waiting for me outside the school gates, and I picked her up and drove straight home. The rest of the afternoon was spent in the garden with my daughter, and it was only as I was getting her ready for bed that I thought again of the earlier incident with the eagle. She was sitting on my knee, sopping wet with a large towel wrapped round her, having just come out of the bath, and she was recounting the events of school that day. As I rubbed her dry I listened intently, making the odd comment here and there.

This was our time, my daughter's and mine. A time for chuckles and cuddles and talking. A bedtime ritual I indulged in thoroughly. That precious hour of closeness, nice soapy smells and warmth.

So I nodded and smiled as I listened attentively to her chatter. Then she said, "And we've been doing birds, Mum, as well."

"Birds? What do you mean, you've been 'doing' birds?" I replied.

Samantha explained how they had been discussing various types of birds in her nature class that afternoon.

It crossed my mind, as I tucked my daughter into bed a short time later, that birds seemed quite relevant today to both of us. And was it my imagination, or did I really hear my unknown "spirit being" chuckle at this thought?

This evening, Wednesday, was my "development" night. So as soon as I'd put Samantha to bed, I got ready for my visitors. There were five of us that night. Besides myself, Irene, Paul, and Mick, I had decided to invite a woman who was a regular visitor to the Friday discussion group.

Adele Campion was a lady who, on first meeting, conveyed the wrong impression. She seemed quite dour, rarely smiled, and had extremely strong views on many subjects. Some may have called her pigheaded; others more kindly would have described her as strong-minded. I liked her, and for many reasons.

I found her openness and candor refreshing, and even though it was well hidden, she really did have a great sense of humor. A little dry, perhaps, but lovely all the same.

Later on, both she and her husband, Phil, became good friends of mine, and at a time when friends were very thin on the ground. If I ever needed help or advice, these two kind people were always on hand.

On this Wednesday evening we five sat in a small circle, not really knowing what to expect, Adele least of all. Mick had requested she sit quietly and not interfere in any way, no matter what happened.

We had begun by asking, as always, for protection and for God's guiding hand. And then we sat and waited.

Slowly I became aware of that now familiar feeling that precedes trance: a sensation of being weighted down by a tremendous but unseen force. My body became a dead weight, but my head felt light and almost weightless.

As usual, I struggled to try to retain control of my senses, and I felt, rather than saw, Mick's reassuring hand in mine. "Just relax," he said, his voice soothing and calming. "Let it happen, and don't try to right it. We're all here to help, just let yourself go."

It took a while before I was able to do as he said, but gradually I let go of my inhibitions, and the trance state was complete.

No sooner was I "out" than I was replaced by the first spirit entity waiting to communicate.

Being only in the first stage of trance, I was able to see and hear all, and as I looked on I was amazed at the transformation my body was making. I watched in fascination as my physical body began to move, slowly at first, as if someone were trying it on for size. Then, quickly becoming used to it, "he" stood up.

It seemed not to be my physical self any longer, being much taller and quite broad set, giving the distinct impression of a male form rather than female.

He stood high in stature and straight, his shoulders set

back and his arms folded across his chest. It was no longer my own physical form that I was looking at, but his.

His very presence was electric and tremendously impressive, but the thing that struck me most about him was the power and energy that seemed to exude from his very being. He was tall and broad, dark skinned, with shoulder-length black hair. And he had the most startling and beautiful eyes. Standing straight and proud, bare chested, with his arms folded, he looked around the room.

Then he spoke, in a voice strong and vibrant with energy, and all became clear.

"My name," he said, "is Grey Eagle, and I am Apache.

"From now on you will know me as guide, teacher, and mentor to your medium.

"Together we will work in spiritual harmony, she and I. Your medium will learn many things, and her progress will be great.

"We will achieve much.

"My little flower is weak and exhausted from her many earthly trials. She needs water, food, and sustenance, which I, as her spirit guide and protector, will give.

"Which I will always give."

Now there are many strange and unaccountable things that happen in the course of a medium's working life. And I would surely lose faith in myself and in my guide if I were to pretend, for the sake of credulity, that they did not.

My new guide had, I had noticed, referred to "his little flower, his rose." But it took a few minutes after hearing this before I realized with some surprise, who it was he had been referring to.

His little flower? His rose?

Yes. His little flower was me. And yes, Mick McGuire did surely watch as I "ate" my words, for as he had told me just a few months before, my spirit guide was indeed an American Indian.

Grey Eagle spoke more. His English was good, with only a slight, undefined accent. His voice held a special quality, firm and strong but at the same time gentle. I was drawn toward him, compelled to listen.

"We know each other, she and I, and yet she will not remember me.

"We who are of spirit have been waiting.

"The time is now.

"We have asked of her a great service.

"She will do well."

So many other things were said that night, as Grey Eagle explained his presence and the need for spirit guides. He also told us of how the dancing Scotsman had been sent on ahead so that the ground could be prepared for the work that was before us.

My guide has often, since that first visit, referred to himself as "the gardener." And once or twice I have been chastised by him, but gently, if I have thought to make decisions concerning certain people around me whom I have to work with.

Two or three years later, when I had set up a healing organization and had begun teaching the art of healing, I remember having problems with a particular class of students, and I decided that perhaps one or two of them were possibly not suited to the work. Maybe, I thought, it would be better for the class as a whole if I asked the more disruptive element to leave.

Grey Eagle, gently but firmly, reminded me, "I am the gardener," he said, "and I will do the weeding."

A few weeks passed without incident, and then within days I had phone calls or visits from more than half my students, all telling me that they were leaving my group for one reason or another.

I was left with a handful of students, and some of them were probably not the ones I would have chosen to stay.

But Grey Eagle knew what he was doing, and all of these students went on to do very well, to learn and to develop spiritually, and to become fine healers.

At first I was in total awe of this amazingly forceful man and wondered why he should want to work with me. After all, I was a novice, a mere beginner, even though I did undoubtedly have a certain talent.

The five of us, Paul, Mick, Irene, Adele, and I, continued to meet each Wednesday evening for my development. Now there was a sixth—Grey Eagle—always present, always teaching. Only I could see him, but all of us felt his presence, his power. It was impossible not to. The very air was electric, and we were all inspired by his strength. Paul said that in thirty years' involvement with spiritualism he had been privileged to meet many spirit guides. But none of them had been as powerfully impressive and commanding as Grey Eagle.

We began, as he had said we would, to work together, and initially I was, or tried hard to be, the perfect student.

Samantha, now almost twelve years old, was well aware of my involvement with the spirit world, although I was careful not to overload her with too much information and would wait for her to ask her questions, as and when her curiosity was aroused, and, I would always try to answer honestly. As a child I was afraid, fearful of those in the spirit world, as I know them now to be, afraid of the unknown, the unknowable, for there was never anyone around who could help me to understand. As my child grew and had similar experiences, for she, too, had the gift of "sensing," though in a much, much milder form, I was able to help her understand those experiences and to take away the fear.

When she asked, I would talk to her about my development and my experiences when in trance, how I felt, what I saw, but I never allowed her to witness trance work, as it would have been far too scary for her to watch, especially when I did my spirit rescue work.

Spirit rescue is necessary only if, when a person dies, usually in an especially traumatic way, that person refuses to accept his or her new state of being. I discovered, as Grey Eagle taught me, that there are mediums who devote their time and energy totally to this kind of work, and in the early days of my development Grey Eagle knew that this would be good experience for me as well as for those in the spirit world who needed this kind of help. So, for a while, as I met each Wednesday evening with Mick, Paul, Irene, and Adele, we too devoted our time and energy to spirit rescue.

The need for spirit rescue is quite rare and can be dangerous and exhausting for the medium both mentally and physically. Not only does the medium, through trance, vacate his or her body and allow a spirit entity to use that body—he or she will also accept that the entity needs to be allowed full and extensive expression of his or her thoughts and feelings. Care must be taken by those who work with the medium to ensure that conditions for this work are favorable. Always I have Grey Eagle's protection, and part of that protection is making sure I have the right people around me when I work. With rescue work it is doubly important that the people who sit with me are sensible, emotionally stable, and able to cope with any eventuality.

The first spirit rescue that Grey Eagle brought to me was a woman who, using my body, began to relive her death experience. All of the souls I have helped to rescue have gone through their death experience a second time. Reliving the death experience helps them fully accept and come to terms with the fact that the return to the earth plane is impossible, that their journey must continue on in another way.

When Grey Eagle brought this first lady to me she was in great distress, struggling with the abrupt and ghastly way she had died. Through me, using my body, my vocal cords, she relived the accident she had had, the fear she had experienced as she'd sat behind the wheel of her car as the truck that killed her approached. She relived the shock at the point of death, as she looked to where her body lay, and realized she had been decapitated. As the most bloodcurdling and chilling scream emitted from my mouth, we realized that it had been this terrible shock that had created a block in her mind and therefore a denial of her situation that had prevented her from going forward to her new life.

Mick and Paul talked to her for about an hour and encouraged her to talk to them. They explained that she had to go forward, that the dark place she was in was of her own making. Gradually she became calmer, more at peace, and much less afraid.

While all of this was happening I had stood to one side of my body, listening and in sympathy with everything I had heard, aware of the immense stress and sheer terror of the woman as she had seen her head cut off. Now I could feel that she was much more peaceful and that she was slowly coming to terms with the fact that it had only been the physical self she had used during her life on earth that had been destroyed. *She* had remained whole.

As I watched from my vantage point I became aware of a gathering of souls, people in the spirit world who had come to escort this lady home. I knew that our work, mine and that of my small group, along with Grey Eagle, was nearly done, that very soon now she would vacate "my" body and continue her journey in peace. By giving her the opportunity to relive her death, and to talk with mortal beings on the earth plane, she had been able to understand that it was time to move on, and she was no longer afraid to do this. She had indeed been rescued from her fear.

Another rescue we did involved a woman who had been buried alive. I have no idea how or why this lady was buried alive, and it was not for me to know. It obviously was not necessary for us to be given this information in order to help her, and I have learned over the years to detach myself some-what from the intrigues of people's lives, information that would only muddle my mind. Again I was fascinated to see how this woman was able to use my body as I looked on, amazed, to relive the trauma of her death. My (her) body writhed about as she tried to claw her way out of the coffin she was trapped in. I too was reliving her death with her, even to the point of seeing the ends of her fingers, broken and bleeding, as a vision came to me of her struggle. Even-tually she too, as with all of those who have been brought to us by Grey Eagle in this way, became calm and found peace, and I was able then to watch as she vacated my body and went toward her loved ones, who had been waiting, to continue her journey.

Grey Eagle taught me that what I must remember is that

we all have a free will and each of us is responsible for who we are, how we grow, and what we become. Through life, each of us is given many opportunities to learn. Our journey is one of discovery. Whether or not we choose to take these opportunities is up to each of us. But we do choose as individuals, we do make conscious choices as to which path of life we walk down. As we go on, past death and into the next world, continuing our lives, we have those same choices, and those who are brought to us for rescue, their choice was to reject the new path that was waiting for them when they first passed through the door called death.

Grey Eagle was a good teacher, kind and patient, never asking more of me than I could give. Never sharp, always caring. And my confidence grew.

For the first time in my life, I was spoiled, nurtured, allowed to believe that I was someone special, for to Grey Eagle I was.

After the healer man had first talked to me of spirit guides, it had occurred to me to wonder whether my father might be my guide. But this was not to be; in order for me to develop my gift, my potential to the fullest, I needed a guide who was a highly evolved spirit being, which Grey Eagle is. Even when he was living on the earth plane, Grey Eagle, born Apache, was a shaman, a wise man, seer, teacher, and healer. Because he was a spiritual leader of his people, he was well qualified to guide and teach me.

There are so many things that I have been taught by Grey Eagle. His wisdom, his understanding, his great compassion, tolerance, and love of others, are so inspiring. As a shaman he has taught me, as only a shaman can truly teach a shaman, of the power of the spirit self, the light of the soul, and how to use this power. We have been together on many journeys, making vision quests, seeking dream visions, and he has taught me to know myself and to some extent to know my future.

The Apache, a nomadic race, were known to be the most aggressive and threatening of the North American Indians, a warrior race and the last of their people to give up their lands and their rights to the white man. They fought savagely to retain what was theirs, so much so that the name *Apache* struck terror into the hearts of many. There are those who would say that it might have looked better for me had my guide been of a different race, born into another culture, one of a gentle and peace-loving people, that that image would be more acceptable for a spirit guide than the image of a fearsome warrior. But I am unconcerned about this, and I am used to the uncertainties of others in respect to my guide, for I know only of his strength and of his gentleness. I know only that his teachings touch my heart and fill my soul with joy. I too am a warrior, fighting for those in the spirit world. So we stand together, my guide and I, side by side in unity one with the other, and I am proud that he is with me.

Working with me as my guide, Grey Eagle leads me down the road of learning, never angry when I fail, always encouraging, never doubting. He has taught me that it is not *what* you achieve in life that is important, only that you try.

Grey Eagle made a promise to me on that first meeting, to give to his little flower water, food, and sustenance, and I can tell you honestly that he has never once deserted me when I have needed him, and I feel his protection and guidance all around me. I know that it will be there for all of my life, both here on the earth plane and also as my life continues in the next world.

This all sounds, I know, like a child's fairy story with a "happy ever after" ending. But my heart is full of love for this man, my spirit guide, Grey Eagle, and it is certain that we will be together, and work together, always.

The Eagle and the Rose.

The
Illusion

When I first began my work as a medium with Grey Eagle, my natural sense of curiosity led me to ask many questions, mostly about my ability to communicate with the spirit world: Was I born with this gift? Why was I born with this gift? How and why did Grey Eagle choose to work with me? I asked whether I could develop that communication further, how I could best serve those in the spirit world wishing to use me as a channel, and of course, how "it" worked. By "it," I meant that natural and easy link that unites and connects me with those external universal forces.

Many of these questions were answered over a period of time, but not easily, for Grey Eagle has taught me that my search for truth must begin from within. The questions that still remain may or may not be answered in time, depending on how much time or energy I am prepared to give toward more discovery.

So many people who come into contact with me and

learn of my gift and of my spirit guide presume that I have an instant and remarkable wealth of knowledge at my fingertips and that if I have a problem, or a need to know something, all I have to do is to ask Grey Eagle and he will spell out the answers to my questions as if he were some great personal encyclopedia especially available for my own use. But it is not like that at all. Part of his role as my guide is to teach me to teach myself, so when I ask my questions of him, his answer is usually, "What do you think?" He can, and often does, help me discover answers, like all good teachers; and like all good teachers, he is always there to listen, to encourage, and to steer me gently along my path. But I am not infallible and have often found myself having reached one conclusion, through some (often) small experience, only to discover that my thought process was too narrow, too earthly, too inflexible, and that I have some major rethinking to do.

Strangely, though, although by nature an inquisitive and curious human being, I rarely have asked Grey Eagle questions that relate to him personally, knowing that he would tell me about himself when, and if ever, he was ready to do so. He is, I have discovered, a highly evolved spirit entity, very learned and knowledgeable, but to describe his place in the universe would be like trying to explain the structure of the universe. With my limited vision, I am able to grasp only the very basics; I know that much of the structure and plan of the universe is beyond my understanding and not at all similar to anything of our earthly world that I have experienced so far. I marvel at the intellect and attention to detail, the precision manifested by the workings of this great and often unseen force of which we are all a part. It is both wondrous and, at times, puzzling to me.

Another thing I have discovered that I know little about is the concept of time. My work has taught me that time in the spirit world is of a different essence from time as we on the earth plane know it to be.

Once, a patient of mine, Colin, who was dying of cancer, wanted me to ask Grey Eagle if he would describe the universe. I was doubtful that we would receive a fulfilling answer but nevertheless asked the question of my guide. He chuckled at my uncertainty and replied, "That's easy, tell Colin it's like holes in a cheese." I relayed the message, expecting Colin to be muddled by this answer, but he simply nodded and told me that Grey Eagle had verified his own thoughts on the matter. I, too, smiled, for I understood exactly what the information meant: tunnels, passageways, some running parallel, some crossing, each in harmony with the other, each a gateway to new life and new learning, full of light and color and discovery. Like holes in a cheese, seeming to have no purpose yet naturally formed. Seeming to lead nowhere yet going everywhere.

There are many who talk on the subject of the universe with great authority. I am not one of them. I am aware that what I know is just a very small part of the whole scheme of things. With my senses keenly tuned I listen in awe and with wonder when Grey Eagle speaks to me of the universe and of our (we of the earth plane) place in it. When he is ready to teach me something, I hear his words of wisdom, and as two souls joining, our hearts touch and I am filled with joy, for his words are always full of hope and bring me great comfort. Yet even saying this, I must add that his words do not absolve me from personal pain and anxiety, for I am human and am here on earth to learn.

Even though I am fortunate to have constant contact and

communication with those in the spirit world this does not make me all knowing and all seeing and above the trials life brings to us all. Those souls, real people, and I see them in supermarkets, on the street, in restaurants, wherever I go, are of our world too. And this gives me the insight to understand that pain, no matter how prolonged it seems to be, is just a short-lived thing that one day, in one way or another, we will overcome. And when I work as a medium and am able to reunite those of us here on earth with those in the spirit world, this knowledge helps me and I know that I can in all truth give people hope of a brighter future.

There are of course times when I might see something in someone's future that is not too good, and I often will be told of future trials that I am able to give good and sound advice on (although I must state here that no real medium will ever reveal anything bad even if she or he sees it); in those cases, forewarned is forearmed. Always, the communication between those in spirit and those of us on the earth plane is advantageous and is a great learning process as well as a great comfort.

I am often asked, How do I see these people, these ghosts from another world? Throughout this book and in the numerous stories I have told, you will see that there are many different ways. But I never see them as ghosts, as flimsy or intangible, as so many people imagine them to be. In fact, I believe from my many experiences that the spirit world is more real, more solid, than this earth in which we live. In truth, ours is a world of illusion. All that seems so solid is yet just a mass: molecules locked together, forming an impression of solid matter that in fact is not solid at all. A "ghost" is seen to walk or to pass through a wall. We presume therefore that the "ghost" has no real substance. Yet we know that in reality it is the wall that is not solid, that has no substance. Could it be, then, that the "ghost" is more real, more solid, and therefore able to pass through the wall because *the wall* is merely an illusion? My belief, through my experiences, is that the world in which we live is but an illusionary world, a world that one day we will leave behind as we travel on toward our destiny and toward reality.

Another question I am often asked when people realize the extent to which I see those in the spirit world is "How do you cope with these people, these 'spirits,' around you all the time?" My answer is simply this: How do you, all of you who cannot see, cope with your blindness, your emptiness?

The story I would like to tell you next is one of many "ghost" stones I could relate and it shows how easily the world of spirit, of reality, can merge and become part of our everyday living.

The term *ghost* is used to describe the apparition of a dead person or animal, a disembodied spirit. The term *poltergeist* is applied to a noisy and mischievous ghost—a ghost seeking attention. And the term *specter* is used to describe a haunting spirit, unsettled and often roving.

This story begins in a remote little village near the town of Brigg in South Humberside, England.

The site is an old sixteenth-century cottage owned by a young man whose brother and business partner used part of the cottage as a studio. The two were successful commercial artists, and although neither young man lived at the cottage, both worked there most of the day.

The cottage itself, small and rather quaint, with its original oak beams, had been renovated in keeping with its character, and as one would suppose with a cottage of such age, it had had many occupants.

When the older of the two brothers, Richard, bought the place, he was taken with the peace and tranquillity he felt there. Having just moved from London, he looked on the cottage as a haven, a place to rest and be himself.

Several months passed and everything was working out well, or apparently so, for all of them. There were one or two little niggles, especially for the two brothers, although they didn't confide in each other or, for that matter, in anyone else.

Richard didn't mention to anyone that he had been awakened in the middle of the night once or twice by someone . . . or something . . . tickling his feet. It was an odd sensation, but he knew he hadn't been dreaming and that what he had experienced was real. Nor did Richard tell anyone about the times when, if he went to the bathroom in the middle of the night, he would see a shadow, that of a man, maybe, cross the landing in front of him.

Each time something like this happened, Richard would shrug it off. It must be his imagination, mustn't it? After all, he didn't believe in ghosts.

His younger brother, Peter, never told Richard, or his partner, Ralph, of the "presence," the unaccountable feeling, so strong at times, of being followed around the cottage. It was too silly and just his imagination. It must be, mustn't it? After all, everyone knew . . . there were no such things as ghosts!

Ralph had had no such experiences, and if either or both the brothers had recounted theirs, he would have laughed outright at the pair of them. It would have been just too ridiculous to suppose that the cottage might be haunted. Anyway, Ralph did not believe, by any stretch of the imagination, in ghosts, ghouls, and things that went bump in the night.

So he was in no way prepared for his first encounter with the spirit world—a world unseen by most and viewed with skepticism by so many.

It was late afternoon, early in March 1989, and Ralph had been working hard in the studio, using a special light box used in graphic design. Glancing at his watch, Ralph realized how late it was, nearly five o'clock, and he had a date that night.

I'll call it a day, he thought. I'll just go to the bathroom, then lock up.

In order to get to the bathroom, Ralph had to cross the kitchen, go through the sitting room, and climb the stairs. Not much of a trek, but far enough for a desperate man— and Ralph was a desperate man. He needed the toilet!

Quickly, he crossed the kitchen and opened the door to the sitting room . . . then banged it shut again in panic.

"What the hell was that?" he asked of no one in particular. Then, laughing at his own fear, he added, "You silly clot, it must have been the light from a passing car, shining through the window." Shrugging, he opened the door to the sitting room once more.

The bolt of blue light, sphere shaped, shot across the room in front of him, seeming to come from nowhere.

Completely startled, the young man stood in the doorway, wondering what on earth it was that he had just seen. Then something else caught his eye . . . and he froze on the spot.

The miniature figure of an old man stood in front of him, by the fireplace, staring directly into his eyes, and was surrounded by a brilliant blue light. He didn't speak to the young man, merely gazed at him intently, a curious look on his face.

Minutes passed, and it seemed to Ralph that he was caught up in some sort of time warp. He felt rooted down, yet strangely peaceful. Everything was so quiet, deathly quiet . . . he could almost hear the silence.

Then, during this deathly hush, the old man suddenly disappeared, seeming to Ralph to shoot straight through the ceiling.

This abrupt movement broke the spell, and Ralph, panicked now, turned on his heels and ran from the cottage, vowing never again to go back.

Later, terrified and shaking, he told Richard and Peter of his experience, and the two brothers opened up and recounted what had happened to them.

Now what? Here we have three level-headed young men, none of whom believed in ghosts or any kind of psychic phenomena. And the mere suggestion of an afterlife would, before this, have sent all three into hoots of laughter.

So what were they to do?

None of them wanted to go back to the cottage . . . none of them wanted to face whatever strange being was in there.

It was the brothers' father who eventually came to the rescue. After listening to the boys' story, he remembered a chance meeting in a cafe in Scunthorpe with a lady who, he recalled, had claimed to be a medium. He also remembered how impressed he and his wife had been as she'd talked with them. She had seemed so ordinary, so down-to-earth, not at all what they might have supposed a medium to be.

Since that time, his wife, the boys' mother, had heard many reports of this woman, all impressive, telling of her seemingly amazing gift. This lady he had remembered was me, so they decided if it were at all possible, to enlist my help.

I listened quietly over the telephone as the boys' father told of the strange happenings and eventually agreed to talk with the boys at the cottage.

This time the three young men were in for an even greater shock than the one they had already had—but one of a much more pleasant nature.

For over four hours I sat with the boys and talked. First I explained what being a medium meant, my beliefs in the afterlife, and the possibilities of communication between the so-called dead and the living. Smiling my understanding of their obvious skepticism, I made it plain to them that they were right to be skeptical. After all, why should they believe a total stranger, who really did seem to talk such nonsense?

I was fully aware, I added, that they needed to see some credentials or, rather, be given some evidence to show that I knew what I was talking about—in fact, that I wasn't a charlatan.

Out first visitor from the spirit world was a gentleman whose hand, he told me, had been badly crushed when he was a young man, and he told me that he was Ralph's grandfather. Because of the information he gave to me, both about himself and his family, Ralph recognized him immediately.

Then the grandparents of the two brothers, Richard and Peter, also came to talk to us and through me were able to give precise evidence of their existence after "death."

Richard and Ralph sat stunned, only nodding their acknowledgment of the incredible accuracy of the evidence given. Peter, the youngest and most emotional of the three, burst into tears as he realized from what I had said that his grandmother, of whom he was especially fond, was not only alive and well, albeit in another world, but at that moment actually with them in the sitting room of the cottage.

All three young men were shocked, amazed, but elated at what they heard. Here was a stranger giving real proof of a life after death.

But now for the real reason I was there. I had to discover the identity of the "apparition" that Ralph had seen so vividly. I also knew that I must, if possible, discover the reason for his visit.

Was he a ghost, a poltergeist, a specter in the night? I doubted it, knowing that nine times out of ten, visitors from spirit were just ordinary people wanting to make their presence known.

I discovered that indeed this specter was just that, for I was able to locate him instantly, and he was more than willing to talk to me.

He was an old man who had at one time lived in the cottage. He had been interested in all of the renovations to the place and had decided to take a good look around.

His interest turned to curiosity when, on one of these visits, he had come across Ralph, or rather the strange object that had sat on Ralph's desk. The strange object that emitted a familiar blue light, and he had been drawn toward it, wanting to take a closer look at the young man, the box, and the beautiful blue glow.

I talked to the old man for quite a while, explaining to him that he had given the boys quite a scare.

"If you visit again," I said out loud, "perhaps you could do it more discreetly."

At this suggestion, all three boys in unison said, "Please,

no, we would like him to visit whenever he wants. Now that we understand, we think it's great."

The funny thing about this story is this: When the old man was describing the strange box to me, he told me how puzzled he had been as to what it was, this odd blue glow, shining out into the night. Was it a ghost, he'd wondered, a ghoul . . . or maybe something that went bump in the night!

This story can lead us to so many more questions than those we already have—questions about parallel worlds, what reality really is, and which is more solid, the spirit world or the world in which we live, we mortals of the earth plane.

There are hundreds of stories I could recount, experiences with so-called ghosts, poltergeists, and the like. Suffice it to say that whenever someone tells you a ghost story, of a haunted house or a shadow in the mirror, don't be so keen to dismiss what they say or presume they are crazy . . . for you see, they could be right!

What is reality? Who are the ghosts . . . those in the spirit world or those of us who are here on earth?

The
Strangled
Lady

All mediums are sensitive. The more sensitive we are, the easier it is for us to "tune in" to those in spirit. I was once told by Mick McGuire, my healer friend, that the price of good mediumship is sensitivity, but at that time I didn't fully understand exactly what he meant. I do now. When I am teaching—helping my students to develop their healing abilities—the one thing I try to instill in them more than anything else is to learn to listen to their inner selves. To make themselves more aware of their thoughts and feelings and, when reaching out into the beyond, to try to "tune in" to those in spirit. In order to do this successfully, they must open themselves up to the thoughts and feelings of those with whom they are trying to make contact. There are many exercises we can do that enable us to become more sensitive, and in a future book I will enlighten the reader, explaining spiritual self-awareness in more detail.

It is really a question of trying to "feel" your way. Very

often, when a medium first makes a communication link, it is not through voice contact or with sight, but more by way of "sensing" a person's presence. Therefore your senses must be finely tuned. Most people can learn to develop these senses; obviously some have greater success than others.

A natural medium has the ability to tune in, using these senses, without ever realizing what she or he is doing. When I first started working psychically it was my natural ability to "feel" my way into the hearts and minds of those who have "passed over" that caused me the most problems. Learning to deal with this in a professional way instead of allowing myself to be engulfed by all the emotion was difficult.

You must now try to understand that working as a medium is a two-way process. If you were using a walkie-talkie, you could talk into it and be heard by the person "on the receiving end," and by the flick of a switch you could hear that person talking to you. Now imagine what it would be like not only to hear on a two-way system, but also to "feel" all of the emotions of the person in the spirit world with whom you are talking, and for that person to feel your emotions, too.

In this next story, I will try to illustrate just exactly what I mean by all of this. I was consulting with Margaret, a young woman in her early thirties who wanted to learn the fate of an aunt who had died in tragic circumstances two years previously.

Even as Margaret was speaking, I heard a voice in my ear say loudly and clearly, "It's Aunt Maudie."

What happened next occurred so quickly, and felt so real, that I thought I was going to pass out.

I felt two large hands wrap themselves around my neck

and press hard. The sensation of being strangled was over-whelming, and my eyes felt as if they were bulging out of my head. As if that weren't enough, I then had the strong impression that my head was being banged against a wall again and again.

Although I had many times had the experience of being "taken over" by those in the spirit world, I had rarely felt such real panic. A terrifying fear spread over me.

These feelings, sensations, and impressions were Aunt Maudie's way of telling me, as graphically as possible, how she had "died."

Somewhere in the back of my mind was one thought: I must stay in control. (The duty of a medium is to give evidence of survival, not scare the daylight out of clients.)

Then Grey Eagle's voice came to me, quietly but firmly saying, "Stay calm, and stay in control."

It was his voice that made me take a grip on the situation, and my mind "shouted" back at Aunt Maudie, *Stop it . . . stop this now! You can talk to me without all this drama!*

Poor Aunt Maudie! She just hadn't realized that what was for her just a way of making her presence felt, and of telling her story, was for me an experience I could well have done without.

After a while I managed to convince her that it would be much easier for both of us if she simply talked to me. If she felt it necessary to describe how she had passed over, then she should do it quietly and not be so enthusiastic in her description.

This agreed, Aunt Maudie began her story.

She had been living with a man, whom she called her husband, for several years, but for the last two years things between them had been difficult. He had lost his job, which had become redundant, and being unable to cope with the new situation, he had started to drink rather heavily. The inevitable happened. Aunt Maudie started nagging, he in turn drank more, she nagged more. It became a vicious circle.

Then, one night, Aunt Maudie's "husband" came home roaring drunk. I suppose you can guess what happened next. Aunt Maudie decided that enough was enough and began shouting at him to get out of the house. Before she realized what was happening, his hands were clamped tightly round her throat. Then, viciously and with great force, he began to bang her head, again and again, against the wall.

Eventually his strength gave out and he let go of the once happy, lively body of Aunt Maudie, which, now limp and lifeless, slumped to the floor.

Staggering into the bedroom, he collapsed onto the bed in a drunken stupor and slept soundly for the next few hours. When, the next morning, he found Aunt Maudie's body lying in the middle of the sitting room floor, he was totally stunned and at first couldn't remember what he had done. He was later to give himself up to the police and was eventually found guilty of murder and imprisoned.

Although Aunt Maudie's passing had been violent and traumatic, she herself had been able, with the help of friends and relatives whom she had met on the "other side," to come to terms with what had happened. She bore her "husband" no malice. In fact, she told me that she felt very sorry for him. Whereas she had had the loving arms of her family waiting to comfort her, he now had nobody, for all his family had turned against him and he was without love.

Emotional upsets leave scars which are, for most of us, the hardest to bear. Aunt Maudie, having lived through this terrifying ordeal, should have been particularly distraught, yet she took great pains to make me understand how she felt so that I could explain to her niece, my client Margaret. Although at first, with the shock of death and then the revelation of a new life, she had been, to use her own words, "a bit of a mess" emotionally, she had had a lot of time to come to terms with things. She had received a great deal of help from her loved ones on the "other side."

"Please," she said, "tell Margaret that I am now well and very happy with my life."

There are, I know, many people who are not only seeking evidence that the people they loved have survived death. They also need reassurance that these people are well and happy. Almost everyone who comes to me for a sitting and who makes contact asks, "Is she [or he] happy?"

During this sitting Margaret was given this message by Aunt Maudie: "I am content."

I have seen Margaret perhaps two or three times since that first memorable sitting, and I know that she feels some peace and has gained a little understanding of life, both on this side and on the "other side."

She told me that knowing Aunt Maudie has been able to forgive her "husband" for this terrifying deed, she has been able to understand that there are always two sides to every story. Margaret now strives to be more tolerant of other people's shortcomings. She doesn't always succeed, but she tries.

There is, of course, a lesson here for all of us. It is so easy, isn't it, to judge other people and their actions, and most of us are guilty of that. Perhaps we should learn to leave the judgment to God and trust Him to decide what is right and what is wrong. Maybe then we too might learn to feel, like Aunt Maudie: content.

In Stephen Covey's book, *Seven Habits of Highly Effective People*, this phrase says it all:
"Be a light, not a judge.
"Be a model, not a critic."

Talks
and
Services

Several months had passed since Grey Eagle had come into my life. Samantha, now twelve years old, was settling down at school. I was working, taking private consultations, never fewer than three a week and increasing steadily, as by word of mouth my reputation began to grow. Money was my greatest problem, and I often cried and fretted and worried when I was on my own, fearing I wouldn't manage—but for all that, life was good.

It was through Mick McGuire that I came to work at the Stainforth Spiritualist Church. He had decided that the time was right and that I was ready to "stand on the platform"— go public.

"Don't worry," he said as he broke the news of this engagement to me, "it's only a small church, and there are never many people there. And besides, I will be right there with you."

Stainforth, although a mere ten miles from where I lived,

was a place I had rarely visited and didn't know much about. I had been completely unaware that it even had a spiritualist church until Mick dropped this little bombshell on me.

Mick continued, "You don't have a thing to worry about," he said. "I'll give the philosophy and all you have to do is give some clairvoyance."

As I knew that I would have to get my feet wet sometime, I nervously agreed to go, consoled by the fact that my friend had stressed not many people would be there to witness my first public appearance.

The fateful Sunday arrived all too soon, and at four o'clock that afternoon, having been jittery all day, I went upstairs, had a bath, and went through to the bedroom to get changed.

Even though my guide had reassured me again and again, I had been on edge all day. I kept telling myself that Grey Eagle would be there and everything would go well, and in some part I had managed to convince myself. In fact, as I sat down at the dressing table to put on my makeup, I was quite pleased with the way I was handling the situation. I was keeping my nerves under control. Or so I thought.

Then I looked in the mirror—and gasped in horror at the sight before my eyes. I was looking at a face that was almost unrecognizable to me.

Huge red lumps had appeared across my cheeks, making my nose look as if it were in the wrong place. My neck and shoulders had developed into a great swollen, salmon-pink blob, and as I watched, more lumps and bumps began forming on my forehead. From my shoulders up I was looking at one great big, blotchy red mess.

Oh, my God! I thought, my heart sinking into my boots. What on earth can I do?

Well, I tried cream, and makeup, then more cream, and more makeup. But the more I tried to cover up the mess, the worse it got, and time was running out.

Eventually, with no more time to spare, I gave up, dressed quickly, and without even a backward glance in the mirror, went out.

By the time I got into the car I looked like a very lumpy red balloon. I drove to Stainforth to meet Mick, all the time muttering to myself and to Grey Eagle that at least I would be noticed, if nothing else.

Mick took one look at my face and burst out laughing, which only made matters worse than they already were. "I knew you would be nervous," he said, chuckling, "but I didn't expect you to be as bad as this."

He had known immediately what had caused the rash. My seemingly calm exterior had hidden my true feelings. I was terrified.

Most spiritualist churches run on a shoestring, and speakers go around the country, working without pay, claiming only traveling expenses. All of the churches I have ever worked in support themselves on a voluntary basis, and this church was no exception. The Stainforth Spiritualist Church building is a very small place, not much more than a barn. It is very easy to miss, as it is set back off the road and insignificant looking to boot. Only when you step in the door and feel the love and warmth inside it do you have any indication that it is a church at all.

When we arrived most of the congregation were already there, about a dozen adults in all, and I was quaking.

Well, I needn't have worried, because things went very smoothly, and I actually enjoyed myself. First of all we sang a hymn, then Mick took over and talked to the small group about his beliefs and how working as a healer had given him a greater understanding of what Christ had meant about loving others as yourself.

I listened intently, forgetting for a time how nervous I was, until he introduced me to the audience. "Here is someone very special with a very special gift, which she would now like to demonstrate to you," he said.

I stood up shakily, very aware that I was trembling and trying hard not to show it. I searched the room for my first communicator, that person in the spirit world who would like to give a message through me to one of our "flock." Soon I began to work, making clear and positive connections with many waiting souls, and my nervousness disappeared as I simply got on with the job that I had been born to do. And the rash? Well, that stayed with me for three or four days.

A few days later I received a phone call from the president of the Hatfield Young Farmers Club. Hatfield is another small village that backs onto Stainforth.

News travels fast.

"Are you Rosemary Altea, the lady who does fortune-telling?" the young man asked.

"No," I replied. "But I am Rosemary Altea who is a medium."

"Ah yes, well"—he coughed—"someone I know has mentioned to me that you do 'this sort of thing' and that you don't charge. My committee and I were wondering if you would be interested in coming to Hatfield to give our group a talk."

"Yes, of course I will," I heard myself say. And then and there we made the arrangements.

I wanted to know how many people he would expect to

come and what age group I would be dealing with. I also tried to ensure that he knew what he would be letting himself in for.

He told me that the membership was mixed, girls as well as boys, and that age varied from fifteen-year-olds to thirty-year-olds. As for numbers, I should expect probably around twenty people to be there.

At that stage in my life twenty people seemed a lot. Putting down the phone, I turned to Mick, who had just arrived for the Wednesday circle.

"Did you bear that?" I asked. "Did you hear what I just did? I've just agreed to give a talk. You will come with me, won't you?"

He laughed. "Yes, of course I'll come with you."

When I arrived at the community center where the talk was to be held, I was amazed to see so many people assembled. At least thirty-five were there, all in their late teens and early twenties. It was also a surprise for me to discover that I had been booked as the "mystery speaker," which meant that no one there, except the committee, would be expecting a medium.

I looked at the scrap of paper that contained the speech I had struggled to prepare, such as it was, and realized how empty the words seemed. Taking a deep breath, I crumpled it up, braced myself, and walked onto the stage.

At first I was very nervous, but courage came, and before long I began to settle down. What really broke the ice, and gave me complete attention from my young audience, was this:

In an attempt to help them understand about mediumship, I explained some of the different ways that those in spirit can come through to communicate. "Sometimes," I said, "I see them as clearly as I see you. At other times I may see no more than a shadow, or I will see someone quite well, but from a distance. There are times," I continued, "when I won't see a person, but I will hear them quite clearly."

I also told them that many people, not just mediums, can often sense the presence of spirit. Then I asked, "How many of you here have felt someone standing behind you?"

Well, I had hardly got the sentence out before the whole place was in an uproar. My audience had taken the sentence literally and were laughing at the thought of "feeling" someone—or anyone, for that matter—standing next to them. The color came up in my face, which seemed only to delight them even more. Of course, it didn't take me long to realize how they had taken what I'd said.

I looked at this group of seemingly unruly kids, who were laughing all the more at my discomfort and embarrassment, and then I began to laugh. Grey Eagle was laughing, too.

"Have you ever 'felt' anyone?" I spluttered to myself, and then this group of young people saw that I, too, was laughing, laughing with them, and they began to clap.

A few cheered, but they all clapped, and it took several minutes before we all settled down and I was able, once more, to continue with the demonstration. From then on I had their complete and undivided attention as I made connections again and again with relatives and loved ones in the spirit world, and we all enjoyed ourselves thoroughly.

In fact, it was one of the best demonstrations I have ever given—many people from the spirit world came through to communicate—and it was one of the nicest groups I have ever had to work with.

I continued with my private consultations, becoming busier and busier, and some twelve months later I received

another phone call from the same Young Farmers Association, asking me if I would please come back to see them
again and do another demonstration.

But this time I was not booked as the "mystery speaker,"
and more than just a few youngsters came for the night out.
There were people of all ages, old and young. Word had obviously gone round, and I found myself with an audience of
about two hundred people, all of them curious about me
and eager to hear more about the kind of work I did.

It was that demonstration that seemed to trigger things,
and before many weeks passed I was inundated with calls.
Requests came flooding in from women's institute groups,
schools, and churches, and I went from strength to strength,
gaining experience all the time. Always Grey Eagle was with
me, always guiding, reassuring, encouraging me forward.

The first school I went to also stands out clearly in my
mind. Mick McGuire had once again agreed to come with
me, to hold my hand. Although by now I ought to have
gained more confidence, I was still very apprehensive about
standing on stage. What if my mind went blank or if I said
something wrong? Worse still, what if those in spirit deserted me, what then? Every time I faced an audience, small
or large, these thoughts raced through my mind, leaving me
feeling sick and jittery.

As we pulled into the school parking lot, Mick remarked
on the number of cars there were, but we were lucky and
found a space. Naively I assumed that all those cars must belong to people attending night school classes, so imagine my
amazement when we were ushered into the hall.

There were well over three hundred people in the place,
all of them sitting there, waiting patiently for the evening to
begin!

I could feel the panic rising in me, and turning to Mick, I muttered, "I can't go in there, not with all those people, Mick, I just can't do it."

But his reaction was completely different from mine. Grinning from ear to ear and rubbing his hands together delightedly, he replied, "Don't be silly. Come on, this is great, just great." And, grabbing my arm, he began steering me down, the center aisle toward the stage.

He couldn't wait to begin.

We had entered the hall from the back, and as we headed forward, faces turned toward us and I could see people nudging one another and hear voices murmuring, "That's her, that's her, that's Rosemary."

This just seemed to bolster Mick's confidence even further, but all I wanted to do was run away.

After what seemed like an eternity, we finally reached the stage, and I remember standing frozen to the spot, with my back to the audience, looking up into space, trying to find Grey Eagle.

"Help me," I begged. "Please don't make me face all of these people. Make a hole appear. Make me disappear. Do something, anything," I pleaded, "but don't make me face the crowd sitting behind me."

But Grey Eagle didn't seem to be listening to my cowardly pleas, and I found myself with no alternative but to climb onto the stage. If I had run, I don't think I would have gotten very far before Mick hauled me back.

The chairman of the Parent-Teacher Association gave me a lovely introduction, and as I stood up to face my audience the applause was warm, sincere, and welcoming.

That should have made me feel better, but it didn't—

nothing could, I was so intimidated by the size of the crowd, and it was with my knees knocking furiously that I began.

It took me less than ten minutes to give my introductory talk, to explain what we were going to do, who Mick was, that he was a healer, and that he would be giving a talk about his work.

I had raced on, my speech almost incoherent as I gave this information, and as my voice began to wobble and my nerve began to crack, I hurriedly handed over the proceedings to him. The audience was a little confused at first by my short outburst, but they soon settled down and gave Mick their full attention.

Gratefully I sank onto the chair, and relief flooded over me. The first part was over, and I had a respite . . . but not for long. Although Mick can talk the hind leg off a donkey, even he would have to stop soon, and after all, it was me these people had come to see. I was the one they had booked.

What on earth, I thought as I looked around this sea of faces, had possessed me to come?

I looked around at my audience again, and again panic seized me.

Oh, God, I prayed silently, Grey Eagle, don't desert me, please. . . . And in that moment I saw him as I always do, whenever I need him or when he needs to communicate with me.

Standing tall and proud, right at the back of the hall, was my guide, looking at me with sympathy and understanding, a smile playing around the corners of his mouth. "Be still," I heard him say to me in a voice loud and clear to my ears, "be calm and listen. There are those in spirit who want to communicate, and they need you."

Mick was forgotten, my audience was forgotten, and my nerves were also forgotten as now I searched for those who were trying to reach me.

Within seconds I became aware of a young man standing on the stage beside me. He was tall and quite good-looking, with strong features and a determined look in his eyes.

"My name is Alan." He spoke quite clearly, the determination in his voice matching the look in his eyes, making quite sure that I would hear what he had to say. "I passed over as a result of a car crash twelve months ago, and I would like to get a message to my wife."

"Can you direct me to her?" I asked him silently, and he pointed to a lady sitting in the middle of the hall.

"That's her sister," Alan told me. "Please, will you help me? I must let my wife know that I'm all right." His voice then broke a little as he went on, "And the kids as well, my two babies."

I listened intently to Alan as he expressed his thoughts and feelings to me, and perhaps I should explain to you, the reader, yet again that I will frequently make communication with those in the spirit world without any outward sign of doing so. I see and hear spirit people in many situations, in restaurants, bars, walking, and so forth. My "visions," as you might call them, are a common occurrence to me. In this same way I see Grey Eagle, when I wake in the morning and throughout my day he visits with me. He will even help with the most mundane chore if I ask him, which I do. I ask him questions like Did I put enough salt in the stew? How long should I cook the roast? Does this need more sugar? My guide is great to have around the kitchen.

When I am by myself, my communication often will take the form of my speaking out loud, but it is just as natural for me to talk to those in the spirit world using thought . . . or mind talk, and this was how I was now communicating with Alan. My developed senses and sensitivity allowed me to "feel" his emotions as profoundly as if they were my own. I was able to hear him and see him as clearly as if he were still on the earth plane, and so the audience at this point was completely unaware that anything "out of the ordinary" was happening.

Mick talked for another fifteen minutes, but I wasn't really aware of him, for I was too busy listening to Alan, who was now very keen to get on.

Over and over, while he was waiting, he would repeat, as if to reassure himself that I could still hear him: "It's Alan, just say it's Alan."

Finally Mick wound up and handed the stage back to me, and as I stood up, the jelly came back into my legs and for one brief moment I felt paralyzed.

Then a firm hand was placed reassuringly on my arm beneath the elbow (only those of you who have experienced real physical contact with someone in the spirit world will understand this), and I was propelled gently down the stage steps to face the eagerly waiting crowd. Grey Eagle was with me!

Once again I heard Alan's voice, and I looked to where he stood, beside a young woman with blond hair. Confidently now, I pointed to this lady and, as precisely as I could, began the message.

"I have a young man standing next to you," I said, "who was killed in a car crash. He tells me that his name is Alan," I continued, but before I could say anything more, this poor woman let out the most dreadful yell and promptly burst into tears.

Every single person in the hall seemed suddenly to sit to attention, some craning their necks to get a better view of what was going on. Apart from the sound of heartrending sobs coming from the lady I had been attempting to give a message to, you could have heard a pin drop. Everyone sat with bated breath, and the air was electric.

After waiting a few seconds, I tried again to give Alan's sister-in-law her message, but she was too upset. I heard Mick's voice behind me.

"Go somewhere else, Rosemary," he said, "and then come back later when she's calmed down a little." That seemed like a good idea to me, so I started to cross the hall to the far side.

But Grey Eagle and Alan had other plans.

When a medium is working and, as in this case, giving a demonstration, he or she is directed by her guide and can't decide herself where she should go, whom she should go to, or what messages to give. And no matter how sensible it seemed to suggest that I go somewhere else, it simply wasn't going to work that way.

"No matter how traumatic and upsetting this may seem to you to be, you must go back and continue with the message," I was told by my guide. "But don't worry, everything will work out well."

Trusting that Grey Eagle would know of the need of this family for a message from Alan, that no harm but only great joy would come from this, I was reassured.

So back I went. "I'm really sorry," I said, "but I'm afraid I have been told to try again. If you would prefer me not to, then I won't, but if you would like me to continue, then perhaps you would say so and we can get on with it."

Tears still streaming down her face, the young woman

looked at me and with desperation said, "Please, please don't stop. I know I'm upset, but this is terribly important to me, and I really would like you to carry on."

So I continued. Alan told me how his wife, the sister of the lady I was giving the message to, had often nagged at him for driving too fast. Many times, he told me, she would say, " 'You'll kill yourself one day, and then what will happen to me and the kids?' "

"Well, that's exactly what happened. I drove too fast round a bend in the road, and here I am!"

Alan went on to say how sorry he was that he had left his wife to fend for herself and his two young children, both under four years old. His main concern was that his wife should know he had survived death, and he was with her, and that he would be helping her and his children in any way he could.

The last message that Alan gave was to his children.

"Please, let them know that I'm not dead, and that I will always be around to guide them. And please," he begged, "please tell my babies that Daddy loves them."

The rest of the evening progressed rapidly and went extremely well. There were many messages given by me to various members of the audience via those in the spirit world. Occasionally the response would be slow because it is not always the most obvious person who has died who wants to give a message. Sometimes it might be a grandmother you know of but have never met because she died before you were born, or it could be the son of a neighbor or friend, unconnected to you in any way, someone who sees you as a way of letting his family know that he survived death and is okay.

There are times when the person trying to reach you from

the spirit world is someone you have never even heard of, but he (or she) will let you know by the things he will relay to you that he knows you. Then he or she will ask that you go home and check with your family to verify his (or her) identity. This is what happened with Martha, a story I relay later on in this book. And of course there were those in the spirit world, like Alan, who were immediately recognized.

Overall the evening was a great success, the response from the audience amazing, and dozens of people came up to me afterward. Some came to tell me how much they had enjoyed it, some to ask for my phone number, and there were also some who came just to look at me. One or two just wanted to touch me, to hold my hand or stroke my arm.

I had, on that night, with the help and love from Grey Eagle and my spirit friends, inspired many, and we had been able to give hope and comfort where before there was none.

Since that time I have given hundreds of demonstrations, both in England and abroad, and although I am often still nervous, I have learned over the years that those in the spirit world ask only that I give my best, for that is enough. Now when I stand before an audience, no one would suspect the trembling beneath my skirts.

The reason I give these talks is not, as most people would suppose, to prove that there really is a life after death. Nor is it especially to give evidence of survival. Indeed, I often begin these occasions by stating that if anyone has come to see me hoping for or expecting absolute proof that what I believe is true, they will go away sadly disappointed.

It would be impossible for me to provide such evidence in the short time it takes to give a demonstration.

But what is not impossible, and what I try my best to achieve, is to give people just enough evidence to make them think. My one hope is that my audience will go away from a demonstration having been given food for thought; that they should then go forward on a journey of discovery toward a new awakening, a new awareness that there is more to life, more to death, and much more to God's plan than we mere mortals see.

All I do, basically, is to sow little seeds, good seeds. To plough the field and scatter the good seeds on the land, and then I pray that with God's help, those seeds will be fed and watered.

What I hope is that the people who come to see me, having listened to what I have to say, will go home wondering, "Is it possible? Could she be right? Perhaps there is some truth, somewhere, in what she says."

And from those questions, maybe just a few will feel the need to find out more.

Ask, and it shall be given unto you. Seek, and ye shall find.

God's
Children

Since time began, psychics, seers, and sensitives have talked of the "aura," the energy field that surrounds not only humans but every living thing, every plant, every tree, every creature on this earth. Many scientists and skeptics have poo-pooed the very idea and laughed openly at those who professed to see this energy field. Then a Russian-born husband-and-wife team, Valentina and Semyon Kirlean, invented a camera that is able to photograph the "aura." This method is known as Kirlian photography. The Kirleans began their work in 1939, but they had to wait to perfect their invention until 1960, when the Russian government made state money available to them.

The "aura," or energy field, manifests above and beyond the surface of the skin and surrounds the human body for a distance of meters. There are many layers, colors, shapes, and patterns to the aura, and the characteristics of the aura change according to the mental, physical, and spiritual, or inner, state of a person. Simply put, the aura is the mirror image of the being.

Then we have the etheric body. The same size and shape as the physical body, but unlike it, the etheric (or spirit) body cannot be destroyed, is more real, more solid.

The etheric body is the one we use, those of us who go astral traveling, and many people around the world who have had "out of body" experiences recount looking down at their physical body while still in body form—this form being the etheric body.

And when we die it is the etheric body we use, the spirit body, that transports us from the earth plane to the spirit world.

There are many kinds of loss—the loss of a parent, a husband, a grandfather, a friend, an uncle, a sister. But for me, perhaps because I have a daughter of my own, the loss of a child seems the hardest to bear. Such a waste of life, I hear people say. And I nod in understanding, even while knowing this to be untrue. For I have spoken with many in the spirit world, children who "died" as babies, some miscarried, some who "died" at birth. I have spoken with adults, grown men and women who had also "died" in infancy but have survived death and, continuing their lives, growing and learning, are happy and fulfilled.

In the spirit world, a world that most of us can only imagine, we continue on with our lives. Children laugh and play, grow and learn. We expand in knowledge, becoming more aware as we do so of the need for the growth of the soul. There is work for us to do in this new world if we want it, and I have been told by many in the spirit world that their lives are active, busy, and very exciting.

How many times have I heard that old, old phrase "Let the dead rest in peace." This phrase implies total inactivity in the "afterlife," something that is alien to most of us. My experience through speaking to countless souls is just the opposite. Continuing life means continuing living . . . in the fullest sense . . . and that is what we do.

Animals also survive death, and for those of you who are animal lovers, or have had a loving and caring relationship with one or more of God's small creatures, I can tell you that many times I have seen animals in the spirit world, dogs, cats, birds, and so on. And once again I am reminded of a sitting I gave to a lady whose name I have long since forgotten, although her session with me is one that I will never forget.

She had come to me as she wanted to get in touch with her husband, who had died, if I remember correctly, very suddenly from a heart attack. I began my search for him, asking Grey Eagle where I should look, and very quickly made contact. But I was amazed at what I saw.

"I'm here," I heard him calling, and looked to the direction of his voice. Then I began to laugh.

My poor client, obviously nervous and a little emotional at the prospect of hearing from her husband, must have wondered what was going on. I quickly explained, hoping that she would understand.

"I have a gentleman here," I said, "but he is carrying two live geese, one under each arm, and he tells me that he couldn't possibly have come without them."

My client burst into tears. "Thank God," she said. "I'm so pleased that they are all safe."

She told me afterward that the geese had been their beloved family pets. "Like children to us," she said. "My husband would often carry them around with him, one under each arm."

There are in this book many stories, all true, all told and written in the way that I would tell them to you if I were sitting with you in your living room. But of course there is more to these stories, and the way they were unfolded before me, than we have room to relate. However, I know that this book would not be complete without at least two or three verbatim transcripts of contact from the spirit world written in detail to give you a better understanding of how I work when giving private or telephone consultations. I thought I would begin by recounting, as accurately as I can, the story of a woman who came to me as a total skeptic.

We'll call her Jean. She was in her early to mid-fifties, and as she sat down her first comment was, "I might as well tell you now, I don't believe in all this stuff."

Very calmly, totally unperturbed, I replied, "'Well, Jean, you don't have to do this. I don't mind giving one less consultation, it is no problem to me at all."

"No, no, now I'm here I'll have a go," my reluctant client replied, "but I warn you, I only came for a bit of fun." And so we began.

R: I am aware of a man standing just behind your chair, tall and slim. I see him quite clearly. He gives me the name of John. He looks to be in his early to mid-fifties.

J: No, I don't know anyone of that name.

R: (I look to Grey Eagle) I am being shown the star sign of Gemini. Are you a Gemini?

J: No.

R: Again, this man John is showing me the sign of Gemini. Are you a twin?

J: No.

R: John is shaking his head. "Yes, yes," he is saying. "I am her twin. I died when I was just a few days old."

J: (Now white and shaking, obviously shocked) How do you know that?

R: Is it true? Are you a twin?

J: Yes, but, but, he died. I had a brother. He died when we were four days old. My parents named him John.

R: He is nodding, saying, "Yes, yes, it's me, John, your brother."

J: But how? You said he is a man.

R: John is explaining how, as he grew in the spirit world, in just the same way you have grown, how he has watched you, played with you. Laughed and cried with you, and shared your life, just as he would had he not died.

J: I don't believe it . . . can't believe it's true.

R: John tells me that when you were a little girl you had blond curly hair.

J: Yes, that's correct.

R: He tells me that you are married now. Do you have girls? (I check with Grey Eagle) He is talking to me about the girls, two girls.

J: Yes, that's right, I'm married and have two daughters.

R: John is telling me that you recently moved house.

J: Yes, this is incredible, that's right.

R: John is talking about the old house and says . . . "Ask her about Charlie. . . ." Do you know the name of Charles?

J: No, that name means nothing to me.

R: I can see and hear John very clearly. He is adamant, he is chuckling and says again, "Ask her about Charlie . . . tell her I'm Charlie."

J: Oh, my God, did he say he was Charlie?

R: Yes, that's right, does it mean anything to you?

J: In the old house we used to joke around. The girls were teenage then. Very often we would go to the bathroom in the morning to find towels strewn over the floor, in the bath, sometimes pushed into the toilet. The girls were convinced we had a poltergeist. They loved him, he made them laugh, they would say. They nicknamed him Charlie.

R: Your brother is laughing as you recount this story. "I'm Charlie," he says very proudly. "I used to throw the towels around and move things. I was trying to get them to notice me," he chuckles. Then he asks me to ask you . . . "Tell the girls their uncle John has watched them growing up, even as he has watched you grow up." He says, "Tell the girls I am their guardian angel, and I will watch over them and protect them always."

J: (Now crying) This is wonderful, incredible. Is he gone now? Oh, no, don't let him go yet. Can I ask a question?

R: (Laughing) Don't worry, he is still here. I still see him. He is just as excited as you are. What did you want to ask him?

J: I don't know. Can he see me? What does he look like, does he look like me? What does he think of the girls?

R: Yes, John says he can see you. He is laughing and tells me to tell you he is handsome. As I am talking to him he has placed his hand on your shoulder and is whispering in your ear . . . "The girls are beautiful. They are so beautiful."

J: I don't know what to say, I'm speechless.

R: John is asking that I tell you he loves you, and he will be with you always. "Tell your mother, our mother, that she will see her son again one day, when she comes to me."

J: He said that? This is wonderful.

R: (I look to Grey Eagle, again, making sure I am hearing correctly) Now John would like to talk more about the girls. One has gone on to further study, I understand. He is talking about exams.

J: Yes, that's right. My youngest girl is taking her exams soon. Will she be all right?

R: Your brother says don't worry. She will do well. She is a bright child.

J: Yes, she is.

R: John tells me the other girl is very unsettled in her life. "She must be patient," he says, "she must learn patience."

J: How right he is. (She laughs) I tell her this all the time.

R: John says, "Tell them I'm alive, tell them I'm alive and that I am happy."

This story goes on, and John has much more to say to his sister, Jean. Jean has been back to see me many times since that first consultation, and she has brought her girls with her, much to John's delight. And as the years go by and the twins get to know each other better and better, and as the girls get to know and to love their uncle John, they all grow in strength. Jean knows that when it is her turn, when she dies, that it will be John's hand that reaches out to her to help her on her journey. And the girls, even though they will grieve the loss of their mother, will have the comfort of knowing she is not alone.

• • •

This next session, transcribed from a tape recording, shows how easily, and in such a relaxed way, people from the spirit world can communicate. This was the second consultation that G, a woman, and M, a man, a married couple, had had with me. The session begins when M's father comes through to talk with him.

R: First of all, I have this lovely man (here). Now I have to say (he tells me to say) that he is very handsome. He has terrific eyes . . . and I think M that this message is as much for your mother as anyone else. (Much laughter here) He is standing just to the right of me, just next to your chair.

He is grinning at me, he tells me that he's handsome (again). I know that he is your father. I have seen him before.

I saw him the other evening in the restaurant. (G and M own a restaurant) Was he a cook, or chef?

M: Correct.

R: He talks of creating dishes.

M: Correct. Can I ask a question?

R: Just answer yes or no. No questions right now. I promise you can ask questions later.

I have asked him specifically if he will give me some evidence for his son. He shows me a watch. A gold watch. It has a chain on it. It is an unusual watch. He tells me it is very special. I don't know what he means by this. Some connection to a pocket . . . you put it in your pocket. I'm not sure what he means by that. It is very special to him, he says.

There is something on the watch, a catch, I think, that flips up or clips open.

M: Yes, there is (I understand).

R: He is holding the watch in his hand and he says . . . "This is me." I feel he would not have been without the watch. He also talks of a ring. A ring kept in a drawer, kept safe. Your mother has this ring. He places his hand on your arm as I am talking to you. He says, "I am with you." He is very emotional, and he says (to me) "This is my son."

He describes his chest, lungs, breathing, and he had problems in this area for a while before he passed over, and it was very debilitating. He says he kept on going despite it.

M: Yes, he did.

R: He says he wouldn't give in and fought like hell.

M: Yes, that's right.

R: He says, "This is my son. I did not want to leave you, I did not want to leave you." He is holding on to your arm. I see him, and over and over he says, "This is my son. Tell him I did not want to leave him."

M: I understand.

R: He is getting very emotional and says that he is so excited to be here to talk with you, and the first thing he now wants to do is talk of your mother (pause) and your sister?

M: Yes.

R: (Now turning to G) I also see a lady standing just behind your chair. She tells me that she is your mother. I have spoken with her before. She has her hand on your shoulder . . . wait . . . I now have a whole crowd of people here (I hope we have more than one tape). Standing next to your mother is a woman who is very small. A very little lady. Her hair is graying. I don't hear her at all. So far she is just watching. I see black lace draped over her head. Now I hear her say, "I'm from the old country."

G: I think I know who that might be.

R: Now I have to come back to your father (points to M). He has waited a long time to talk to you and is a little impatient to get on.

M: Okay, okay, that's great.

R: Your father tells me that you have been very apprehensive about doing this (communicating) and that even this morning you nearly backed out.

M: (Laughing) Yes, that's true.

R: He tells me that you are a little nervous about what you might hear. He places his hand on your arm and says, "Don't worry, we will be fine, just fine."

Now, once again, he talks of your mother. The feeling I get from him as he talks now, describing your mother as lively and active, living a full life, is unusual in that the emotion, the caring, and the love for her is so strong. He talks of her tears and her pain since his passing and of her struggle to stay bright. Tell her that he is often with her in the night when she cries, and that he sees her pain. She sees him, she knows that she sees him.

M: I will.

R: He says, "We were inseparable." He grins. "She organized me."

G & M: (Laughing) That's absolutely right.

R: He is a very emotional man, and it is sometimes hard to hear what he is saying. "Tell her she is the best wife and mother. Tell her I love her."

M: (Also emotional) I'll tell her.

R: Your father is talking about a new venture and (I know M's mother is an author) says there is a new contract signed. Do you understand?

M: Yes, totally.

R: Your father says, "This one will be even better than the last."

M: Good, I hope he's right.

There were so many other things that M's father talked about, too much to recount here and many, many personal details. We finished the sitting in this way.

R: I can hear your mother quite clearly (this to G). She is giving me the name of Patti.

G: That's my sister, Patricia.

R: Your mother is calling out, "Tell her happy birthday, happy birthday."

G: Oh, yes, my sister just had her birthday.

R: Your mother says, "Our greatest of God's gift is our children. They are precious to us. Send them my love." Then . . . "That gift is not taken from us when we die. We still see you. We surround you with our love."
  She talks about your ear. That you have had a problem with your ear. (This, a question from me)

G: Yes, I have always had problems with my ear, since I was small.

R: Your mother says she will send you healing. (Pause) Now M, I bear your father again. (He then describes, in detail, the areas and building in which he began his first business)

M: Incredible. That's so right.

R: (Again, as always, I check with Grey Eagle, who confirms I should continue) Your father talks of the company and of your plans to expand. (Do you understand what he means?)

M: Absolutely.

R: (Much advice given here) Then . . . "It will expand and do well. I will be watching."

Now he talks in rhyme (this is symbolic); tell me if I confuse you.

Around three years ago a big bad wolf came and tried to blow down your bricks and mortar. (Do you understand?)

G & M: (Laughing) Yes, we do.

R: And he huffed and he puffed, but he couldn't blow the house down.

G & M: (Much laughter and nodding here) Yes. Oh yes.

R: And then the wolf tried again. The house did not blow down but shook a little.

M: It surely did.

R: You looked around and saw some cracks in the walls of the house, and then began streamlining. This has to be done, your father says, and must continue.

M: I understand.

R: (Much more is said now about the company) Then . . . "I know of the plans . . . don't worry, everything will work out fine. There will then be more expansion." (He elaborates)

M: That is correct. I understand fully.

(Again much more is said. M's father talks of G & M's children, giving many personal details of their lives. Everything is understood.)

R: Now, M, your father would like to give you a special message (he says). To walk in God's way is to walk hand in hand towards that light which you know is there, and that light is representative of goodness and of truth, and of love. He shakes his head, and he tells me that you need no teaching, for you have been walking this way for a long time. He tells me you are good people. Genuinely, and from the heart, live your life to the full and have no regrets. For you need have no regrets.

As I am talking to you, M, he has moved around behind you and he puts his arms around your shoulders. His head is very close to yours, and, as in the old days, he says, he gives you a hug.

G, your mother is holding you and stroking your face (I see all of this). They are all crying, but your father, M, is very quick to point out that these are tears of joy. Joy in a coming together and of an understanding that we don't die.

"Never be afraid of this" (dying), he says to tell you. "Your apprehensions were unfounded. Never be afraid that you will lose me, for I will always be with you." Then (with a twinkle in his eye), "I will be with you at the game tonight" (football). "I can't promise anything" (he laughs) "but" (pointing to Grey Eagle) "maybe he can."

(Much laughter here from all of us.)

R: He (M's father) continues. "Be thankful for the love, the joy, and for the light. It is yours and we share it with you.

"I love you, M," I hear him call this clearly, I hear him call, "Be strong, and know that I am with you always."

This consultation with M and G lasted for just over an hour and a half, and there were, as in most of my sessions with those in the spirit world, many, many incredible details. Sometimes such trivial and seemingly unimportant facts, but many of a much more profound nature—all, however, designed in one way or another to show that even after death we are still involved, as much as we want to be, with those we have left behind.

R: I am aware of a young man standing very close to you. He is in his early twenties. He tells me that his death was very sudden, very quick. He was a baby, just a few months old.

Rita: (Crying) I lost my son. He was four months old.

R: He says he could not breathe. A cot death, I think. There was some confusion as to why it happened.

Rita: Yes, that's right. It was a cot death.

R: I see the initial *C.*

Rita: His name is Christopher.

R: I hear Christopher say, "This is my mother."

Rita: (Now crying again) Is he okay? Is he happy?

R: He is very eager to talk to you. To let you know that he is around you and that he has survived death.

Rita: I know he is often with me. Not a day goes by that I don't think of him.

R: I have asked him to give us, if he can, some more details, either about himself or about you. I hear the name Alan. Is there someone with that name?

Rita: My husband's name is Alan. Christopher's father.

R: Your son is talking to me about flowers. Yellow flowers. Some real, some silk?

Rita: (nodding and smiling) Yes, yes. I understand.

R: Then he shows me what looks like a romper suit. A baby's romper suit. Yellow. I also am being shown a small soft toy. I think it's a rabbit. No . . . wait . . . now I see the romper suit again, and stitched on the suit is a rabbit. The suit is yellow. Does this mean anything to you?

Rita: Christopher is describing the little romper suit he was buried in. It had a rabbit stitched on the front. We had yellow flowers on his coffin, and every year, on his birthday, when I visit his grave I take yellow flowers for him.

R: "Tell her I see her," Christopher says, then . . . Christopher is showing me a photograph in a silver frame. I can see this photograph standing on some kind of dresser. Next to it, in a vase, I see yellow flowers. Christopher tells me the flowers are silk. "They are new," he says. "They are new."

Rita: Oh, Rosemary, he really can see, can't he? I bought the flowers only a few months ago. They are in a vase next to his baby photograph.

R: Christopher would like me to tell you that he has grown, and is a man now. That he visits you and Dad often. He talks of "his" drawer. And he is describing to me how you often sit on the bed, he says, open "his" drawer, and take "his" things out to look at them. He tells me how you cry so much because you have lost him.

Rita: Does he see me? Really?

R: In the drawer, Christopher's drawer, there are his baby clothes, wrapped, he tells me, in polythene.

Rita: Yes, that's right.

R: Also there is a bag full of cards. I think from what Christopher is saying that they are christening cards. (He then describes many other things in the drawer.)

Rita: (Crying and laughing at the same time) He really can see me. He really is there. Oh, Rosemary, this is amazing, wonderful.

R: (Smiling gently) Your son wants you to know that he did not die. He wants you to know that he has grown, that he is happy, and that one day you and his father will see him again.

Rita: Rosemary, I don't know what to say. Thank you. Thank you. I don't know what to say. (Crying now)

R: I am just pleased that your son was able to get through to you. He has waited for such a long time. I see him, and can hear him clearly. He would like to give you just one more message.

Rita: Oh, yes! Oh, please.

R: "I love you, Mum." I hear him say this clearly. He says again, "I love you, Mum. I am always with you. Tell my dad I didn't die. No more tears. Tell him that I am alive."

I had met Rita while visiting a patient, Mark, whose story is also in this book. She was one of Mark's nurses, and although I had seen her there previously, this was the first opportunity that Rita had to ask me about healing.

It was as she began to ask me questions about my work that I saw him. He had been waiting for his opportunity, knowing that if I could, I would help him.

I knew that it was no coincidence that she, the nurse, was there. I knew too that he had planned it this way.

Twenty-two years is a long time to wait for a son to finally be able to talk to his mother. And for me, it was a privilege to be able to say to the nurse, "Rita, your son Christopher is truly alive, and is with you always."

She had already made an appointment for herself and her husband to see me and was calling now to see if I could change it to a different day. I was about to say no, but something in her voice caught my attention.

"It seems impossible that day," I said. "Is there a special reason?"

"Yes," she said, sobbing. "It is my son's birthday."

"Well then," I said as gently as I could, "we had better find the time. You will have to come later in the day, but if you can manage that, then I'll see you both."

Now it was June 21. The couple seated opposite me, in their mid-thirties, waited anxiously for me to begin. I do not remember their names. It is only their story that I recall.

R: (Beginning the sitting very quickly) I have a young boy wishing to communicate. Small, with dark hair. A little shy. I hope he is going to talk to me. (I ask him to tell me who he is.) "I'm Robert." (I hear him.) "I'm sith today." (I laugh, knowing that he means that he is six today.) "It's my birthday."

She: (Crying) Yes, his name is Robert, and he is six today.

He: (Anxiously) Is he all right?

R: Please, don't ask questions, not yet. I want Robert to talk to me. (Now I ask Robert, if he can, to tell me how he died. Gently and with great patience, I encourage him to talk to me.) "I was on my bike [I say this to his parents], and a car came fast round the corner and skidded into me. My head hurt, but only for a little bit, then I came here."

They: Yes, that's right, that's how he died.

R: Robert says, "They keep crying, and it makes me cry, too."

She: Oh, no, please, we don't want him to cry.

R: (Very gently) Don't worry, he doesn't cry all the time. But he misses you, too, you know. (Then, laughing) "It's my birthday, I'm sith."

They: Yes, that's right.

R: (As I work I see Grey Eagle standing close to the child, helping, encouraging him to talk to me—I continue, relaying the boy's messages.) He tells me that he was just four years old when he passed. Is that correct?

They: Yes. He was out playing, just outside the house. Quite safe. A car came around the corner too fast, hit the curb and bounced up onto the footpath. Robert was killed instantly.

R: He talks to me now about his brother and sister.

She: Yes, that's correct. We have two other children.

R: Robert tells me you are having a small birthday party today. He is quite excited. He tells me you have made him a birthday cake. I have asked him if there are any candles on the cake. He nods and I see him clearly. He is holding up six fingers.

She: (Crying) My baby has seen his cake. (Turns to husband, who is also crying) This is wonderful. I can't believe it.

The sitting continued, with Grey Eagle helping Robert to communicate. It lasted a long time, and Robert talked to his parents of many things. Because the accounts of his accident, birthday party, and many other things were so accurate, his parents were convinced, as I was, of Robert's survival after death. They will continue to celebrate his birthday, but now, even though there will always be sorrow, there will be joy in their knowing that he is still a part of them, still a part of their lives, growing happier and content, assured that they know he is alive.

I had visited Hong Kong many times and had many clients in the Far East. One of these was a lovely lady named Celia. It was on one of these visits that Celia and her husband, Bruce, came to see me for a consultation and many family members came through from the spirit world to talk to them. Bruce's grandmother was a particularly strong communicator, and through her they were given a profound and moving message that they were not to understand for some time—a message that helped them greatly when tragedy struck their lives.

Some twelve months passed, and I was back in England. The telephone rang one Sunday morning, and it was Celia.

C: Rosemary, is that you?

R: Yes, who is this, please?

C: (Calmly) You probably don't remember me. I know that you see and talk to so many people. (She then explains who she is.)

R: Yes, of course I remember you. What can I do for you? (Although she sounds calm, something in her voice tells me that she has to make a great effort when speaking to me. I know immediately that there is a problem.)

C: Rosemary (now struggling for control), there has been an accident. My son. Yesterday. He slipped and fell into the river. We have had such heavy rains here. All the rivers are flooded. The current was strong. (Now crying, still struggling for control) My son is missing. I know he's dead.

(I feel Grey Eagle draw close to my side. I talk to her, try to calm her, and even as I do so I see her boy. "My name is Michael," he says, and I wonder how I tell her what I see. She cuts into my thoughts.)

C: I don't know, Rosemary, if you can help me, but I have to know if he's safe. I know he's dead. I feel it. I know that it is a lot to ask of you, but could you just ask someone up there if my son is safe?

R: (I hear him call to me. "Tell her I'm safe. Please. She must know that I'm safe.") Is his name Michael? (I ask this tentatively.)

C: Yes, oh yes! Is he safe?

R: I have a young boy here, Celia. He is around eleven years old. I can see him quite clearly. (I describe him.) He tells me his name is Michael.

C: Oh, thank God. He's safe, he's safe.

R: He tells me he was carried downriver.

C: Yes.

R: This is puzzling. He is talking about the waterfall. He says he was carried to the waterfall. Does this make sense to you?

C: Yes, yes. The river leads into a huge waterfall, which goes directly into the sea.

R: Michael is talking to me. He wants you to know that he did not go into the sea. (Now Michael shows me, and just as if I were watching a home video, the picture unfolds before my eyes.) I see first of all not a large river, more a stream.

C: Yes, that's right.

R: I see Michael sliding down the bank. The bank is soft and crumbles. His body is carried downstream, and now . . . I can see a huge waterfall. (Celia is now sobbing, and I ask her gently if she would like me to stop.)

C: No. Oh, no. Please, Rosemary, I need to hear this.

R: Michael is describing what happened as he reached the edge of the waterfall. I can see his body as it goes over the edge. But wait . . . Oh, this is wonderful. Michael says, "Tell her, tell my mum . . ." As his body goes over the waterfall, I see Michael. I see him leave his body. He seems to fly upward. I hear him say, "I flew like a bird, up, up, up. Angels came to fetch me. They carried me, up, over the waterfall, to fly like a bird. It was bright. A bright light shining. They (angels) took me into it, and now I'm safe. Mum, can you hear me? I'm safe."

C: (Still crying) Thank God, thank God. Oh, Rosemary, thank you. You don't know how you have helped me.

A few days later Celia called again. She had been listening to a tape she had made of her sitting with me in Hong Kong, prior to Michael's death, when her husband's grandmother had come through to give them a message.

"My husband's grandmother had talked to us about God and about the ways that God can help us in our lives. But one thing she said to us that we did not understand at the time. I'm sure she meant for us to know now. We were told, 'God may sometimes ask of us a blessed sacrifice, just as He asked of Christ. A sacrifice we may find so hard to give, so painful will it be. But remember what I say to you. When God asks this of us, there is a reason. We may never know what that reason is. But God knows. And when He asks of us this blessed thing, He gives us the tools to cope, the strength to survive.'

"You cannot know, Rosemary, how hearing this makes me feel. I play the tape over and over. It comforts me greatly. I know that Michael's death was meant to be. For what reason I do not know, but I know that he is with God, my blessed sacrifice, so painful to me. But I know that he is where he belongs, where he is meant to be. I talk to him every day. I feel he is with me. I know that he is safe."

There are many reasons why people here on earth are "good" or "bad." Some of us are "good" or "bad" because we enjoy our lives better that way. Others perceive that living a "good" life will earn them brownie points, that somewhere God is watching and keeping score. Living life in a "bad" way is, for some, an open act of defiance to a God they perceive as a judging God. Others might say, "Well, what is the incentive for being good when I don't believe in God?"

But life is not about being good or bad or earning points. Life is about learning and about the discovery of the soul and the needs of the soul. And "good" or "bad" can simply be a right or a left turn on the path which leads to that discovery. Life is not about earning a place in heaven. It is enough for the soul that the life of the soul continues on. That the soul grows stronger.

Throughout this book you will read stories of survival after death. Each tells of a journey, a breakthrough, and the embracing of the light. But do we all journey toward the light? Does God accept us all? Even those who have committed evil deeds?

It is my belief, based on my experience, that the answer is *yes.*

I do not believe that anyone who wishes to be embraced by the light is ever turned away.

We, of course, do have that choice. Each of us—even, I believe, those whom we might judge evil or bad. For if a bad person seeks to go toward the light, then he seeks forgiveness, he seeks to learn of truth. If he did not, he would not see the light, would be blind to it But when an evil person chooses the light, the suffering and pain that he has inflicted on others is nothing compared to his own suffering and plain, which is tenfold. For when he stands in the light, that light forces him to see, to recognize, his own wizened soul . . . his own mean spirit.

There are those who believe that if you commit suicide, you go to a dark place. I do not agree. If those suicides need the light, they will be shown the way. The only dark place is within them. My experience shows me that even they, those who have been so confused while on the earth plane, will be taken, by angels, God's messengers, into the light. When I talk to them, those unfortunates who have been so muddled, they often tell me of their new environment, of their learning and of their growth, which is not always easy for them.

I have spoken with many in the spirit world who, prior to their passing, did not believe in an afterlife, who believed instead that being dead meant no more life—no more anything. Each time, I hear them express their surprise and delight upon discovering survival after death.

Anyone, everyone, can, if they choose, go to a good place. There are no doors that stay closed—no barriers, except those we choose to erect ourselves. There are no heavenly judgments, only the judgments that we ourselves must make as we look at the kind of life we have led, the kind of person we are. Each soul judges its own self. If a soul wishes, it can refuse the light and, closing its eyes against the world, will find itself in a dark place of its own making. As if donning a shroud, it will wander through dark passages and nightmare places, haunted by its own thoughts, lost and alone. But the shadows of the soul are its own and are there only because the soul chooses it to be this way.

And how do I, the medium, see?

With every part of my being. Sometimes as if I am looking at a distance. Sometimes so near that I can reach out easily and touch people.

And, what do I, the medium, see?

I see people. Not spirits: people. For when we leave the earth plane, we take with us the etheric body, the same size and shape as the physical self. The etheric body, indestructible, becomes the vehicle by which we continue our journey.

And how do I, the medium, sense?

By becoming more sensitive. By "tuning" in. I send out my thoughts. They are received. Those in the spirit world respond, send their thoughts out to me. We communicate.

And how do I, the medium, feel?

I feel them draw close to me. I feel . . . sense . . . their emotions. Thought waves bounce back and forth. It is a two-way process. Their thoughts touch me, some knowing part of me. I become as one with them.

And how do I, the medium, touch?

I talk to my guide. Grey Eagle places his hand on my shoulder. There is real pressure there. His hand strokes my cheek. I feel the sensation. I place my hand over his. I touch him. I watch, as often, when communicating, someone from the spirit world will touch . . . place a hand on a shoulder. Stroke someone's hair or cheek. Brush away tears. I watch as those in the spirit world embrace my clients in this way. I see them touching us.

And how do I, the medium, hear?

Sometimes in just the same way that I would hear someone "living." Sometimes I hear . . . through my skin . . . sound waves . . . seeming to seep through my skin.

And what of my emotions, I, the medium, and what of how I feel?

My emotions bubble and ferment. My sensitivity makes it impossible for me to remain passive and untouched. I feel sadness and pain, and oh, such deep, deep sorrow. But I feel happy, and I laugh a lot. It is impossible not to, for there is oh so very, very much joy.

I talk to so many people in the spirit world, so many different races. There is, unlike our world, no language barrier between them, no communication problem that cannot be overcome. My work is so varied. I have worked with the police. With priests and with ministers of the church. With the rich and with the poor. With the famous and with the unknown. And all are known. And all are known. For God sees all. He sees the living and the living "dead."

And I, the medium, find great joy in what I do. For I understand, truly, that we are all known. That we are all "God's children."

PART III

Case

Book

In my work as a medium I realize that, more often than not, the small and seemingly insignificant details give the most powerful proof of life after death. Those small details make each person's life different from that of their neighbor. And it is usually these details that give the most startling evidence of survival to friends and loved ones.

The following ten stories comprising this case book are examples of how—sometimes in a complex, sometimes too simple, but oh so clever way—those in the spirit world show us that they are *alive*.

When I first began my work as a medium, I explored every and any explanation I could think of that might dispute spiritualism. Never once did I doubt God, nor did I ever doubt the existence of another world, a world I knew one day I would be part of. But I did doubt myself and my abilities to make contact with those who had already passed on to that world.

In all honesty I cannot say, during the early days of my development, that thoughts of the possibility of mind reading didn't enter my own head. Of course they did!

When searching for the truth about life after death, or life after life, as I prefer to think of it, it is necessary to distinguish between the real and the unreal. To be able to determine what information is right and what is not right.

These stories leave no doubt.

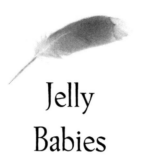

Jelly
Babies

Mr. Dearest sat patiently, waiting for his session with me
to begin. Within seconds I saw a man from the spirit world,
about five feet nine inches tall, a little on the stout side, in
his early sixties. He told me that his name was Alfred and
that he was Mr. Dearest's father. With the help of Grey
Eagle, he explained that he had passed over as a result of a
massive heart attack, and that although his passing seemed
very sudden, he had had heart problems for some years prior
to this.

Mr. Dearest was very close to his father and was overjoyed
at this information. But just when I thought that things were
going well, I was given a message from Alfred to give to his
son. It was a message so strange that I thought I must have
mistaken what I heard.

I asked Alfred to repeat the message, and laughing at me,
he said it again.

I looked to Grey Eagle again, then I exclaimed, "Oh, Alfred, I can't say that! Your son will think I'm crackers!"

"No, he won't. Just tell him what I said."

I looked again at Grey Eagle, who was nodding and smiling, reassuring me that I had heard correctly.

I went back to Alfred. "Are you sure?" I asked.

He laughed again. "Just say it," he said.

So I did.

Mr. Dearest listened intently as I gave the message: "Jelly Babies."

He nearly fell out of his chair in astonishment. The message from his father could not have been more simple, clear . . . or effective.

Later, after we had finished the sitting, Mr. Dearest told me the significance of "Jelly Babies." He explained that when he was a young boy, his father, Alfred, used to take him everywhere with him, and in his pocket he always carried a packet of Jelly Babies.

Alfred was hooked on them.

As he grew older, my client also developed a passion for these sweets, so much so that ever since his teenage years he too always carried a packet with him wherever he went.

"Look here," said Mr. Dearest, and pulling a packet from his pocket . . . he offered me a Jelly Baby!

Martha

There are many stories I could recount which illustrate that what a medium does is not mind reading, but rather a kind of telepathic correspondence similar to mind reading, applied to bridge the void that divides our world from that of the spirit world.

In this book there is room for just one, and it concerns a young man in his mid- to late twenties whom I will call Colin.

The main reason Colin came to me was that he hoped I would be able to make contact with his girlfriend, who had been killed tragically in a car accident. She was only twenty-three years old when she passed, and she and Colin had been making their wedding plans.

He wasn't at all sure that he believed in life after death but felt that he would not be able to rest easily until he had given his girlfriend the opportunity to make some contact with him . . . if, that is, she had really survived.

In Colin's mind he had decided that "if" there was such a possibility as survival after death, he would get his proof in the way he wanted it.

However, it didn't work out at all in the way he hoped or thought it would. In fact, I don't think it had even occurred to him that the proof he sought might just come in another way.

With no trouble at all and with no hesitation, my visitor came through from spirit. A rather stunning lady in appearance, she wore a long gray dress and a straw boater with a black headband perched on her head, and in her hand she held a small book.

In a clear voice she spoke to me: "My name is Martha, and I am related to Colin's mother."

Everything I saw and heard was so distinct, and confidently I relayed this information to Colin.

Imagine, then, my surprise when he said in a voice that portrayed his disbelief, "I know no such person as the one you have described. In fact," he continued, "I know with absolute certainty that there has never been anyone in our family by the name of Martha. And definitely no one wearing a long gray dress and a straw boater."

I looked back to Martha, who, hearing what this young man had said, just smiled a serenely knowing smile, one that spoke of patience.

"Tell him again," she said, "and don't worry if he doesn't understand you, he'll learn."

I told him again, but again Colin was adamant that if there had ever been such a person in his family, he would have known about her.

He was obviously deeply disappointed at the appearance of Martha, as he had made up his mind that if anyone should make contact from the next world, it would be his girlfriend.

Colin was now firmly convinced that I was a fake, so it was difficult trying to explain to him that we don't always know many of the people who come through from spirit to talk to us. Gradually, however, his disappointment and disbelief turned to amazement as I began relaying messages from Martha concerning Colin's family.

Martha was particularly explicit about his mother and his mother's family, giving such startling evidence about them that it was clear, even to Colin, that she knew the family very well.

At one point we discussed Colin's job, and chuckling, Martha said, "Tell him how smart I think he looks in his uniform," and before I had a chance to repeat what she had said, Martha showed me a picture of Colin wearing a naval jacket and—dare I say it?—a funny hat.

Poor Colin. When I told him all of this, he was amazed. Everything that Martha had said he understood. The information he had been given was so accurate that he could not deny the evidence of his own ears.

So how did it work? How could I, a stranger, tell him not only about himself, but about the people around him—and with such accuracy?

These were questions that he now had to ask.

Finally the sitting was over. Colin switched off the tape recorder and only then told me, and nearly in tears, how the visit to me was for the sole purpose of getting in touch with his girlfriend.

All I could say to him was that it was not up to me as a medium to decide who the communicators would be, but I tried to assure him that what be had been given must be what he needed.

He was a little angry at that and said quite firmly that he knew better than I that his need to talk to his girlfriend was much greater than his need to talk to a woman he had never even heard of—a woman, in fact, whom he doubted had ever even existed.

I, too, was upset when Colin left, feeling his hurt and disappointment. "Had I missed something, some small but important detail?" I asked Grey Eagle. He assured me that I had not and that everything would work out well, but still I was unhappy. I should have had more faith.

A few hours after Colin left the phone rang, and his voice came on the line.

"Rosemary, I must see you. It's desperately important."

After leaving me, Colin had gone straight to his parents' house, and they had all listened as he played the tape recording of his session with me.

His mother, shaking with excitement, had raced up the stairs and a short while later returned, carrying a very old photograph album.

Colin watched, his heart thumping wildly, as his mother thumbed through the pages. Then, with a look of triumph on her face, she pointed to one particular photograph. Colin hardly dared to look. There, smiling up at him from this dusty old photograph, was a lady, short and plump, wearing a long gray dress and a straw boater on her head with . . . yes . . . a black band around it!

Colin's mother, with tears in her eyes, looked at her son, and in a voice full of emotion, she said, "That lady is my grandmother. She died, Colin, before you were born, and her name . . . her name is Martha!"

Had Colin, at that time, been given evidence of his girl-friend's passing and her subsequent survival, I am sure that he would initially have been overjoyed.

But because he was such a doubting Thomas, he may eventually have come to the conclusion that the evidence he had been given was perhaps nothing more than mind reading.

His great-grandmother Martha had come through unexpectedly, determined to prove, and in a way that would be impossible to dispute, that there really is such a thing as life after life.

Elizabeth

Having read Colin's story, you might assume that all those in the spirit world who wish to make contact through a medium find it as easy as Martha, Colin's great-grandmother, did. And for many it is that way. But there are those who struggle for one reason or another, as this next story will show.

It was 1982. I was on my own and struggling to survive. I had been left with no money, enormous debts totaling thousands of pounds, and a house I couldn't afford to run. Every penny I could earn counted, as it literally meant, for Samantha and me, the difference between eating and not eating.

Cash was something I needed desperately at this time, and although it would be nice to think that spiritual wealth is the only important thing in life, unfortunately this just isn't so.

We live in a material world, in which we all have to earn

money, one way or another, to pay our bills, to feed and clothe us and our families.

Mick knew this, and so he arranged for a group of people to meet, ten in all, for what he called a "clairvoyant party."

He didn't tell me about it until all the arrangements had been made, and at first I was angry, and refused to do it. But when he mentioned that I would be paid a small fee . . . well, I was sunk. I needed the money.

Mick had known what a desperate state my finances were in, and this was his way of putting a little cash in my pocket.

The "party" was held one evening in the home of Elizabeth. I was nervous and on edge. I didn't like the idea of working this way, able to give only fifteen minutes of my time to each person.

Mick had come with me and suggested that we all join together in prayer before I began. We joined hands, and as Mick prayed everyone bowed heads—well, everyone but me, that is. I took the opportunity to study my potential clients.

But as I watched, I had a vision: garland upon garland of tiny rosebuds began to appear all around the room, strung across the walls in long loops. They decorated the room in the most beautiful way, and they were a gorgeous shade of pink.

It was by no means the first time that Grey Eagle had given me strength and encouragement in this way. In fact, I remember one time I was very unhappy about a patient of mine, Margery, who had died of cancer. I could not help wishing that I had done more for her, although what more I could have done I did not know. As I was pondering on this one day, I became aware of a bright light shining out to the left of me, and as I looked toward it I saw the prettiest sight:

masses of pansies, such lovely flowers, the markings on the petals looking so much like faces. They all seemed to be smiling at me as they waved about in the breeze. As soon as I saw them I was reassured and smiled, knowing instantly that this vision was given to me by my guide so that I would know Margery was safe and happy, for you see, pansies were her favorite flower.

So it was, as in a vision, I saw those tiny pink rosebuds in such a spectacle of color that I felt a reassurance and immediately became less nervous. What a lovely way Grey Eagle had chosen to let me know that he was with me! It never occurred to me that there might be another reason for the gift of flowers.

Despite my apprehension and misgivings about the evening, everything went well. I sat in the dining room, and one by one the ladies came to me for their sittings. For every one of them, evidence of survival after death was overwhelming.

It is always a pleasure for me to make communication links such as these. Over and over again I listen to the evidence from those in the spirit world, not only of their survival after death, but of their constant and continuing interest in the people they have left behind. Help and advice is given on so many subjects, even the most trivial—advice that is always valuable, whether it has to do with business, health, children, education, or affairs of the heart; advice made even more precious because it comes from those in the spirit world, who see so much more clearly than we, who are so easily blinded by emotions.

It is also possible for those in the spirit world to see farther ahead than we can, and so they are able to give help and advice concerning the future. And part of my pleasure comes from being able to help set people on the right track, of watching as enlightenment dawns with the knowledge that not one of us is alone and without aid of one kind or another. Even when the outlook for the future is not so good, those in the spirit world are able to give good and sound advice that will often ease a situation, giving strength and hope that the bad times will not last forever.

The last of my sittings that evening was with the hostess, Elizabeth. I had sensed how nervous she was immediately, so without delay I began.

Already I had begun to listen to Grey Eagle, and, as always, he told me all of the things about her that I needed to know. As with all of my sittings, my first communication is with Grey Eagle, but I had still not looked at her as I said, "Now then, what's all this nonsense about rats?" And as I sat down in front of her, I looked into the most startled pair of blue eyes I had ever seen.

Continuing, I repeated, "Rats, you have been having dreadful nightmares about rats, haven't you?"

Speechless, she nodded, and huge tears bubbled up in her eyes and ran down her face.

I reached out and gently patted her hand. "Well, shall we see if we can help you?"

Nodding again, she whispered, "But how do you know, how could you possibly know about my dreams?"

"A medium is someone who quite simply is able to talk to the dead," I explained. "And I know about your dreams because my spirit guide, Grey Eagle, has been talking to me about you since you first walked into the room." I smiled a reassurance and then, "Now, shall we continue and try to see if we can find out what this is about?" And of course we did just that—and we addressed her phobia.

A few days later I heard from Elizabeth again, and we arranged a time for her to see me.

"I'd like a proper sitting," she said. "Last time your guide spoke to me. Now I would like to get in touch with my mother. I really need to know if she is all right and, of course, whether or not she really survived death."

"There are no guarantees that I can make contact with your mother, or that she will want to speak to me," I said. "I can only guarantee that I will try. The rest is up to her."

This agreed, Elizabeth came for her first "proper" consultation, but although I did have several communicators, I didn't manage to link at all with Elizabeth's mother.

Disappointed, but determined to try again, Elizabeth made another booking.

Three sittings later, four attempts and four disappointments, and still I could not seem to form a link with the one person Elizabeth felt she needed to hear from.

"It's no good," I sighed, after the fourth time, not liking to admit defeat myself, "I'm afraid I just cannot seem to find the right wavelength. Perhaps it would be better if you found another medium. Your mother might find it easier to communicate through someone else."

In tears, she shook her head and tried to reassure me that it didn't matter. I suppose she was tying to convince herself as well.

I made us both a cup of tea, and we sat in silence for a while. Then, in an effort to cheer her up, I said, "Come on, it's not the end of the world, you know. How's Katie? Tell me how she's getting on." Katie was Elizabeth's handicapped daughter.

Immediately her face brightened and she began chattering

away, telling me that her daughter had just been found a place at a special school and how well she was doing.

Nodding and sipping my tea, I listened as my friend chattered on. Then suddenly I became aware of another lady also nodding and smiling as she listened to Elizabeth, standing quietly by her chair.

Not only did I see her clearly, I also heard her quite plainly as she turned her attention to me. "Hello," she said, "my name is Doris Rose. I'm Elizabeth's mother. I've been trying to get through to you for ages."

Without thinking, and cutting straight across what Elizabeth was now saying, I repeated what I had just heard.

The cup of tea that Elizabeth had been holding went sailing into the air, and a look of joy spread over her face. Bobbing her head up and down, she gasped, "It is, it is, that's my mother's name! Rose is my maiden name, Elizabeth Rose, and my mother is Doris Rose."

Doris Rose told us many things that day and was able to provide her daughter with the much needed evidence of her survival after death. She told of her illness, her cancer, and her struggle to fight it, how she thought she had succeeded until the day she became ill again and died shortly after. Describing that moment of death, Doris explained to me that her daughter had been sitting by her bed, holding her hand, and that the last thing Elizabeth did for her while she was alive was to wipe her face and dry her tears.

When I asked her why it had taken so long, so many attempts on my part, to get through to her, she explained that she had been too nervous.

"Every time I tried," she said, "I just got the collywobbles, and couldn't do it. I hope you'll forgive me and understand." And of course, I did.

Then Doris went on to tell me how she had tried to let her daughter know that she was there on my first meeting with her.

"As you now know, my surname is Rose, and my favorite flowers are roses, and Elizabeth knows that more than any others, the tiny pink rosebuds, like the ones you saw when you first went to her house, are the ones I love the most.

"Grey Eagle placed garlands of them around the room for me, and I was hoping that you would tell her about them, but you didn't."

The garlands of roses I had seen when I first went to Elizabeth's house. Oh, such a beautiful sight—but I had missed the significance of them. Such a small point, seemingly inconsequential. But because I hadn't seen it, I had failed to see Doris Rose.

Thank goodness that Doris and her daughter had persevered. Thank goodness they had kept on trying.

"If you had told her, I'm sure that my daughter would have realized the significance and known that I was there," Doris said then. "Perhaps," she concluded with a smile, "you could tell her that I will always be with her when she needs me, always."

So many of us, when first coming into contact with a medium, are nervous or even downright afraid. Not sure what to expect, afraid of the unknown.

Many in the spirit world are also afraid. What if I can't hear them? What if I misunderstand them? It's a bit like being afraid of messing up on an important exam.

Thank goodness Doris Rose overcame her nervousness, her fear of not being heard. And thank God for the many in the spirit world who helped her, and others like her, to break through the barrier and make contact.

Suicides

Fear is an intangible thing, an illusive and insidious emotion that can cause destruction and devastation, if allowed to grow. Fear of death is common in most of us to a greater or lesser degree, for isn't death considered that great "unknown"? But there are many who equally fear life, fearing failure to achieve, to compete with their peers, or even to take that next step that will lead them around the corner, again to come face-to-face with the "unknown."

There were times in my life when I have feared living, times when I feared dying, and it is my knowledge of the spirit world and the workings of the universe that enables me to dare to be. To dare to be my own self with quiet confidence, able to go forward to meet the many challenges that life itself brings.

The ancients, the grandfathers, American Indians, believe that each of us as individuals owns the power of the universe, to do with it what we choose. And they, like others from ancient cultures, had an understanding of the spirit world and all that the universe encompasses, living their lives enlightened by that knowledge, embracing life and also embracing death as it came to them, joyfully and proud. *Hanta Yo!*, Ruth Beebe Hill's book about the Native American Indians, offers a phrase that expresses perfectly what I mean: "continual habitual spirituality."

One of my aims, working as a medium, is to teach you, all of you who would come to learn, in the same way that I too have been taught, to give you a greater understanding that life is an adventure, a learning experience that, if embraced, will help us grow. In that growing we can discover the spirit self and truly know who we are. Death is a door that we all must walk through, and it is that spirit self that, discarding the physical body, will take us on to continue our lives, learning and growing as we go.

I am fortunate in that I was born with, and have recognized, the awareness of the spirit world. I am of the universe even as I live my life on the earth plane, and with that knowledge I have been able through time to face my fears and to deal with them. Consequently my life has become more and more fulfilled and fulfilling. Truthfully I cannot say if, at the moment of my death, I will race through that door willingly, for even now the thought of leaving behind friends and family, particularly my daughter, saddens me. I feel sure that I will be apprehensive about the journey to come, but I know it will take but a moment before I see the light that will show me the path that is mine to follow. I know too that I am, even on the earth, walking a path that is also lit if I care to look. This makes me unafraid of life.

Unfortunately, those whose stories I now tell did not have such understanding, were not awake to the joys of life, to the gift of life that is so precious; so, blindly, and with fear in their hearts, they walked their path here on the earth plane in darkness and alone. These people chose to take their own lives.

Suicide is a difficult thing to talk about because, unlike all other causes of death, it is self-inflicted. A person decides, using his or her own free will, to end life. But the fact is, and these people usually discover this too late, that life continues. There are those, both in the church and some concerned with the legal system, who consider suicide to be a terrible crime. I know that some of you who read this book will be of the same opinion. To say that it is a crime or not a crime is to be judge and jury. So I will leave all the judgments to God and simply tell the stories, all of which are true. But I will change the names of the characters to prevent inflicting more pain on the relevant families.

The lady who had come to me for a consultation sat facing me, waiting for me to begin. She appeared to be in her early thirties, although I discovered later that I had underestimated by about ten years. Despite the obvious pain showing clearly on her face and the desperate look of sorrow in her eyes, she was very attractive. I realized instantly that here was a woman in deep distress.

When her friend had rung two weeks earlier, begging me to see her immediately, my first reaction was to say, "I'm very sorry, but I have a waiting list of at least six months." But even as I was saying this, Grey Eagle was telling me something different.

"This one really is urgent," he said. "Will you please fit her in?"

I looked through my diary, and sure enough I had one afternoon off—the first in weeks!

So here she was (we'll call her Mrs. Jones) with her friend, the one who telephoned, standing in the hall. You don't have to be psychic to tell when someone is greatly troubled, even though that person may be putting on a brave face, so it was quite apparent to me as I ushered them into my study which of the two ladies was my client.

Working as a medium can sometimes be a great strain, and occasionally before a sitting, especially if I'm feeling tired, I will ask Grey Eagle, "Can we make this an easy one?"

Although he always helps me, and without him I would be completely useless, he doesn't have a magic wand, and if he did have, he wouldn't use it. It is impossible to "make" anyone who has passed over communicate. It has to be an action born of free will.

I have yet to see or hear about anyone who can "raise the dead," and I would never use methods of any kind that might force someone in the spirit world to talk to me. All a medium can do is hope, wait, and be patient.

I have rarely contacted a suicide with anything other than some difficulty. Those I have spoken to who have killed themselves, for whatever reason, all have one thing in common. There is always a feeling of tremendous reluctance on their part to make the first step toward communication. It is a reluctance born of fear, fear of rejection by those they love, those whom they have left behind to face the hurt and pain of living.

Within minutes I was aware of a very strong presence in the room but could neither see nor hear anything that might help me establish a contact. Patiently I waited, asking over and over, "Where are you, can you talk to me?"

But nothing.

Those who have taken their own lives often need a

tremendous amount of coaxing and encouragement. I always try to show my love to them and let them see that I care. For me, the trick is never to lose my patience, to remain gentle and caring, and to gradually gain the confidence of the person in the spirit world who is waiting to communicate. It is also necessary to remember that the client is very likely becoming more and more nervous.

Mrs. Jones was no exception, and as the minutes ticked by she became very edgy. I reached out and patted her hand gently, smiling reassurance. "Patience," I said. "Just try to relax and leave the rest to me."

Still we sat and waited, and it was more than thirty minutes later—it must have seemed like forever to Mrs. Jones—when I saw him. He was a young man, very slim, not very tall, and I guessed he would be around eighteen years old.

In fact he was twenty. At first he was extremely nervous, scared that he would be rejected, and scared that he would make a mess of the sitting. I let him know that we weren't in a hurry, that he could have as much time as he needed; slowly and carefully, and with Grey Eagle's help, I managed to build up a rapport between us. Eventually the link grew stronger, and then I heard his voice. It was faint at first, but as he became more confident, I was able to hear him more clearly.

"My name is Ricky," he said. Then, pointing to my client, Mrs. Jones: "And that's my mum."

He then promptly burst into tears, so relieved to have finally broken through the barrier that separates our two worlds. After he had calmed down and become familiar with his new situation, he began to speak. Little by little he overcame his initial reluctance, and I found that he was quite a forward young man with a great personality.

Most people on the other side, when talking to a medium for the first time, feel the need to talk of their last memories of life on earth. These memories, of course, include how and why they have passed over.

Ricky was no different, and very soon he was giving me all the details.

Often when I communicate with those in the spirit world it is like sitting in front of a very large TV set, and in just the same way that I would watch a home movie, those in the spirit world will relay their information with words and pictures. As I carefully take note of the vision, the "movie" that I see, the person in the spirit world with whom I am communicating will give his or her own narrative. I may be shown a picture, a "photograph," of how they looked when they were younger. Sometimes there will be many voices, many people, family and friends, wanting to be heard. Other times I may hear just one voice. This was how it was with Ricky.

He began by describing the garden shed, a big old place that had stood for years in the grounds of his family's house. The house itself was old and brick built, and as Ricky talked about it, I realized that he had a tremendous affection for the place, as had his mother. He talked about the tall trees surrounding their land and how in winter it was a very spooky place to live, the wind whistling through the trees, making them creak ominously.

It is always difficult for suicides to talk about how they have passed, because often these people who take their own lives still don't really know why they have done it.

Suicide doesn't solve anything, even in sickness, because the problems we all encounter during our daily lives, no matter what they are, are there as obstacles to be climbed over.

Problems will be there whatever we do, wherever we are, whether we are on this side or the other. It is how we deal with them, our state of mind, that determines how big or small, or insurmountable, these obstacles become.

Dying doesn't change who we are, and Grey Eagle assures me that our problems go with us.

Positive thinking is something we should all try to achieve, and putting an end to our lives on this side simply means that we must achieve this state of mind in another place. Our lives on the earth plane have a purpose, and that purpose is to learn, to discover as much about our true spirit and the importance of our own spirit selves as we can.

Ricky must have realized this, and his struggle with himself would have been made all the more difficult knowing how badly his family had been affected by what he had done.

As Ricky relayed his story, I of course told Ricky's mother all the things that he said. Tears rained down her face as she listened, nodding but silent, indicating that she understood what I was saying but unable in her grief to react further.

Quietly I listened while Ricky repeated the description of his home, letting him know that whatever he wanted to say, whatever he wanted to do, was fine with me, even if it meant repeating things a dozen times to make sure we'd understood.

Each time Ricky mentioned the garden shed he would become agitated, and I began to suspect that it was this detail more than any other that had some bearing on this young man's passing. Step carefully now, I thought, as gently I steered his thoughts back to the shed, hoping that he would tell me more, and eventually he did.

He told me of the day—his last one on this side—when

he had decided to end it all. For years he and his father had been at loggerheads. They only had to look at each other for the rows and arguments to start. On the day in question he and his father, as usual, had had a row. Not a big one, not much more than a spat.

Afterward, for some reason known only to himself, Ricky fetched the shotgun his father used for shooting game and went down to the garden shed.

After sitting alone for some time, staring up at the rafters and listening to the wind whistling through the trees, he put the gun to his head and pulled the trigger. Many hours passed before his body was found, and the police were called in, as foul play was suspected.

The agony and pain his family sustained during this time, and since, is indescribable. The terrible burden of guilt had been laid upon their shoulders, and nothing will ever be able to remove it.

It is unlikely that anyone who had not experienced similar traumas can imagine the atmosphere that now hung heavily in the air in my small study. I had repeated, almost word for word, the story Ricky told, and his mother was now weeping uncontrollably before me. It is a hard thing for a mother to come to terms with the fact that her son had been unhappy enough to kill himself, for whatever reason. Mrs. Jones could not understand why Ricky had done such a thing, and I'm sure she never will. Her son was unable to help her because he did not know, either.

My job was now to assist this young man in his aim to prove to his mother his survival and to let her know that despite everything, he was well.

"All right now, Ricky," I said, aware that Ricky would

connect with and understand my every thought and respond to it, "tell me about yourself, your interests, the things you remember most about your life on earth."

Pretty soon I learned that Ricky had been a very fashion-conscious lad. Clothes were important to him. It was the pair of shoes that he had bought just a week before his death, and that he described so accurately to his mother, that gave the ultimate evidence that her son was very much alive. These shoes were very special, being very light in color and extremely "unserviceable," and Ricky thought they were wonderful. This particular fact brought a watery smile to Mrs. Jones's hitherto unhappy face, and soon she was laughing as her son described some of the antics he used to get up to. Relaxed now and feeling much more sure of himself, Ricky was able to relate many incidents to me, both about himself and his family.

He did not tell me that his suicide was a mistake. I felt his remorse, his concern for his family, and I know that his growth, the growth of his soul, will be impeded in some way until such time as he comes to terms with what he did. But I also know that there are many in the spirit world who will be willing to help him overcome his difficulties—and when he is ready for that help, all he will have to do is ask.

I would like to be able to end this story happily, but, of course, I can't. Although Mrs. Jones has been back to me many times since that first sitting, and is surely convinced that her son is alive, there still remains a sadness. Both she and her husband live in darkness, for the light has gone out of their lives; but every now and then the light is rekindled as they remember that the boy they love and who is lost to them is still there somewhere.

It was the trivia, the small but so significant details, that showed Mrs. Jones her son was still alive. His light burns ever bright in another world, and they know that one day they will be with him again.

Confronting
Death

Like Ricky, Peter had also taken his own life. As I talked to him, I discovered that he had had a morbid interest in death, and at every given opportunity he would try to discuss, both with his family and his friends, what it would be like to die. Every time he brought up the subject, however, he found the same reaction: no one wanted to know.

Both his family and his friends would shut him up. They thought him strange and would refuse to listen, telling him that his curiosity was unhealthy.

One day, not long after Peter passed over, his parents decided to sort out their son's belongings and straighten up his bedroom, in the hope that they might find some clue, some indication, a reason why they had lost their boy.

They couldn't believe what they found. Numerous books and magazines stuffed on shelves, in cupboards, under the bed, and all of them concerned with the same subject—death.

His inquisitiveness had turned into obsession, which had subsequently led him to take his own life.

It happened one night, after his family had all gone upstairs to bed and were safely out of the way. Peter sealed all the windows and the door of the living room, using masking tape. To make sure he would be comfortable, he placed some cushions on the floor in front of the fire.

Ensuring that the gas fire was on full force and, of course, not lit, this eighteen-year-old boy lay down on the cushions and went to sleep.

It became more and more apparent to me as the sitting progressed that the only reason Peter had gassed himself was simple curiosity. He had felt a need to know, to find out one way or another, what death was really all about. The more he had read about the subject, the more questions he had wanted answered.

But no one he knew had been able to help; indeed, it had seemed to Peter that no one wanted to help. So he had come to the conclusion that the only way to satisfy his curiosity was to find out for himself.

Unfortunately, even as I talked to this confused young man, his regret at having committed this futile act was obvious. It saddened me enormously.

If only our society did not treat the subject of death as taboo, as forbidden territory, as something morbid. Perhaps if Peter had been able to talk out his thoughts and feelings with someone who could have understood why he felt as he did, he might not have felt the need to take such an extreme step.

If only we could all talk more freely about the one thing in our lives that is, more than anything else, inevitable, without being afraid, then maybe this boy, and others like him, would not have developed such an unhealthy interest. Perhaps his understandable and perfectly natural curiosity would have been satisfied.

This truly was a case of curiosity killing the cat.

All of us, at some time in our lives, have discussed the wonders of nature, and we marvel at how every living thing produces and reproduces. But no one prepares us for death or seems willing to discuss the "facts of death."

By law, our schools' curriculum in England must include some education concerning childbirth and the use of birth control methods. This topic is discussed widely by children and parents, and indeed most of us encourage our children to ask questions. And if we, as parents, are unable to answer perhaps some of the more searching inquiries of our offspring, we can always find out. There is always someone we can ask.

So why is it that even the mention of death, the most natural, the most inevitable act we will all perform, frightens many people?

I have come across those who will talk about it in hushed voices, but definitely not in front of the children. And I have met those who just refuse to talk about it at all. Few people can speak of death and dying, especially in relation to themselves or those close to them, as a perfectly natural happening.

One of the main complaints of those who themselves are dying, and having to endure the pain, both physical and mental, of long illnesses, is that even their families, those closest to them, cannot bring themselves to broach the subject. I've heard my patients tell of how embarrassed they become, even when out shopping, because friends avoid them. One man told me that he felt like a leper when walking down the street because people he knew would see him coming and cross to the other side or hide in doorways.

"Death isn't catching," he complained, "but most of my friends act as if it is, and avoid the very mention of the word."

In all cases, when I have come into contact with people who are terminally ill, I am asked the question: "What is death?"

And in each case, I can only explain my beliefs. There is no such thing. "Death" is merely a transition from one world to another. We are all in some respect afraid of the unknown, but those who are about to "die" are being made through circumstances to face their fear. And they need to be able to express their feelings.

Then there are the families of these people—husbands, wives, children, who every night will offer up a silent prayer to God, declaring to Him, and only Him, the dreadful fears that torment their minds. What of their needs?

At the age of twenty, I was one of these people, having suddenly been taken seriously ill. I knew nothing of the spirit world or of Grey Eagle at this point in my life, had never given any real thought to death or life after death, as I had not experienced losing anyone close to me. But suddenly I found myself facing the realization that death was ever near. I had undergone extensive major surgery, which I had known very little about at the time, as I had been too ill to take much notice of what was happening to me.

At this time I had been living in Market Harborough, a small market town about two hours from London. I had been married just six months, and my husband came in from the garden one day to find me sitting on the toilet, of all places, screaming in agony.

He managed, with great difficulty, to lift me up and then carried me through to the bedroom and laid me on the bed. The doctor came, and for a week I lay, in a semiconscious state, totally drugged. Three times a day a nurse came in to give me muscular injections, using a needle that was inches long, and to give me my medicine.

Toward the end of that week it became obvious that I was getting steadily worse, and when the doctor called that Sunday evening, he took my temperature and found that it had soared up to 106 degrees Fahrenheit.

I was rushed to Kettering General Hospital, where, even though by this time it was the early hours of Monday morning, the specialist was waiting to see me.

His name was Dr. Phillips, a very professional man and an eminent surgeon. He was to be responsible for my life over the next eighteen months.

For the next week or so I underwent various and extensive tests, many of which were, to say the least, extremely unpleasant.

For four days after my first operation I lay in a coma, oblivious of the care and dedication of the doctors and nurses around me. On the fifth day I came round, and I can remember Dr. Phillips sitting on the bed and holding my hand, trying to explain to me what he had found and what he had done. The tests prior to the operation had shown a problem with the left kidney, and what that problem was exactly became apparent only during surgery. My kidney was malformed from birth and unable to function properly. The tube leading from the kidney to the bladder had wasted and was useless. Several stones had formed in the kidney and had tried to pass from the kidney to the bladder, pushing against the wasted tube, creating the terrible pains I had had. My surgeon continued, explaining that he had worked on the kidney and was hoping that he had repaired it. Also he had replaced the wasted tube with a type of plastic tube, a delicate and difficult operation, he said, but he was hopeful that it would work.

Because I was very young, and still very ill, it was not until some time later, when I was fully conscious and had time to think, that I realized just exactly what was happening to me.

Fear is a funny, often indefinable thing, and it can hit you at the most unexpected moments. For nearly twelve months I knew, I experienced, what being scared of dying really meant.

I had been receiving postoperative treatment, which meant that two or three times, each week, sometimes more often, I traveled between Market Harborough and Kettering, some ten miles, to the hospital, and this went on for several months.

Then one day Dr. Phillips broke the news that I had developed a serious infection that they were unable to treat, probably resulting from the length of time I had been on the operating table. It was imperative, he said, that I undergo more surgery before the infection spread too much.

Still weak from the last operation and all the treatment I'd been having, I sat in his office while he and his second in command drew little diagrams that were supposed to show me what they were going to do. He told me that he wanted to remove the kidney before the infection spread to the right kidney, and they needed to perform the operation quickly.

In a daze I listened, feeling as if I weren't really there, as they explained the dangers. It would be dangerous if I left it, and it would be dangerous if I didn't, I was told. There was only one course of action to be taken, so back into hospital I went.

Outwardly I put on a brave face, and my husband and friends gained confidence from the fact that I would survive, because I seemed so positive about it all.

Inwardly I was a quivering jelly, knowing there was a strong possibility I would soon meet my Maker, and I prayed strong and silent prayers, asking His help.

On the day I was taken down to the operating room for the second time, all my determination to be brave crumbled. Three male orderlies surrounded my bed as I waited to be wheeled away. I had had my premed and should have been nicely relaxed, even sleepy. The doctor approached me with a needle in his hand, and I knew that this was it.

Everything would have been fine if it hadn't been for one of those very nice orderlies, who at that precise moment leaned down toward me and gently and quietly whispered in my ear, "Don't you worry, sweetheart, if you open your eyes and see a bottle of blood hanging next to you. It will be because you are going to need a blood transfusion."

Now I understand that this kind man meant only to help and reassure me, to prepare me for what was to come. But the effect it had on me was startling.

Letting out a terrified yell, I tried to leap off the bed, only to find myself pinned down by the men in white coats. The struggle that ensued is one I will never forget. I fought like a tiger for my life, kicking, screaming, my arms flailing about, struggling to break free.

The fear inside me grew like a living thing, a wild animal, and as it grew it spread through my body and through my mind. Consuming all my thoughts and all my senses, it raged on, and through it I found superhuman strength. Biting, kicking, and punching, I almost made it off the bed, but then, for a split second, I must have paused for breath.

The doctor seized his opportunity; quick as a flash he stuck the needle into my hand, and I went out like a light.

Needless to say, I survived the operation, although it was a long time before I was fully recovered. Years later I still had nightmares about it all, and I would wake up sweating, the memories vivid in my mind, and the fear of death, like a wicked serpent, would rear its ugly head again.

There is an old but very true saying: "A problem shared is a problem halved."

If only I had understood then that putting on a brave face isn't necessarily a good thing. And if only I had realized that my husband and his family were as scared as I was, I am sure I would have been able to cope with my situation in a much better way than I did.

The effort it takes to be brave, not just for yourself, but for others as well, is tremendous, but like the old saying— perhaps effort shared is effort halved.

Learning to talk openly and freely about the facts of life, and the facts of death, may initially prove difficult, but with right thinking it's not impossible. And to encourage our children to ask questions so that we can deal openly with their curiosity is a sensible and down-to-earth way and could save lives.

Many young people, like Peter, have been inquisitive about death and afraid of life, and they have been unable to express, to anyone who understands, how they feel and what they think. To them, suicide seems the only alternative to life, and unable to overcome temptation, they try it.

So the next time any of you are asked by your children, "What happens when you die?" please don't brush things under the carpet or pretend you didn't hear. And don't be afraid to say that you don't really know. Kids can cope with that, but they can't cope with being ignored. Talk to them, and more important still, let them talk to you.

If we can all listen to each other, I am sure that many of us would feel relieved to discover that our thoughts and feelings, and our fears, are shared by many others.

Peter, while communicating through me, was able to show his family that he had survived death. What a pity that he didn't discover a way to communicate sooner—while he was still on earth.

Coach
Crash

When a person decides to take his or her own life—to commit suicide—it is, of course, such a great tragedy. But a choice was made, a conscious choice, by that person, to end their life.

What happened to Mrs. Smith in this next story reflects God's choice of how tragedy can strike at the happiest times, when life is at its sweetest.

The coach, full of passengers all enjoying their continental holiday, had been traveling for a few days, taking in the breathtaking sights during the day, stopping each night at a different hotel.

On this day, the mood on the bus was light and happy, everyone chattering, while the tour operator pointed out various places of interest and gave a commentary of the history of the towns and villages they passed through.

No one on the coach could possibly have suspected, on

that warm and sunny day, that their lives were soon to be shattered—for some, completely.

How could any one of those people have guessed that, before this fateful day was over, some of them would feel the cold hand of death upon them? And others would be seriously injured?

The first sign or warning that told them something was wrong came when the passengers heard a loud bang that sounded like a small explosion. But it was too late to do anything about it.

One of the tires had burst, sending the coach careening and screeching across the road.

Bodies were flung into the aisle and across seats. There were ear-shattering screams as people were flung into the air, to land broken and bleeding over the bodies of others. A few people died, and many were injured, some quite badly, in this terrible and traumatic accident.

Mrs. Smith and her husband had decided on a coach tour of the continent because it seemed to them the best and most reasonable way to holiday abroad.

They were a happily married couple with one son, now a teenager, who was old enough to stay at home with relatives. It was their first holiday together, on their own, for quite a number of years, and they had been looking forward to it for a long time.

As the coach thudded to a standstill, the screams stopped, and all that could be heard was the sound of people moaning and crying. Dazed faces, bewildered and stunned, gazed around at the chaos before them, unable to grasp the horror of the events that had taken place within the last few minutes.

Mr. Smith, stunned and confused, managed to pull himself shakily to his feet. His first thoughts were of his wife, and he searched frantically around the bus. He turned to where they had been sitting, a hundred years ago, it seemed, holding hands and sharing the thrill and excitement of their wonderful holiday.

Little had they known that they were also sharing their last moments together.

Mary Smith lay sprawled across the floor of the coach, and as her husband reached her side, he saw that the back of her head was broken and bloody.

She must have been thrown when the coach overturned and had hit her head. Death had been instantaneous and virtually painless for her, but for her husband . . . he was to feel the heartache and pain of losing her in such a way for the rest of his life.

Immediately, as I had started to work, Mary Smith made herself known to me, and I saw and heard her quite clearly. She was not very tall, with a neat figure, fair hair, and a warm smile. It was she who had described to me the chaos on the coach and all of the incidents that had led to her passing. I then asked Mary what else she would like to tell me, and without hesitation she said, "The funeral, I'd like to talk to you about the funeral." And to my amazement, she started chuckling.

"Ask him," she said, pointing to her husband, "just ask him about the funeral. What a shock he had, oh boy, what a fright!"

She was still laughing as, perplexed now, I asked: "But, Mary, can't you tell me, explain to me, please, what you mean?"

Shaking her head, Mary was adamant. "He'll know what I mean, just ask him."

Well, I was in a predicament now, wasn't I? I could hardly say to this poor man: "Your wife's splitting her sides laughing about her funeral." Not when Mr. Smith sat, broken and desolate, hoping to hear words of love and comfort.

But Mary, undaunted, went on. "Tell him that I'm laughing, and tell him I thought his face was a picture, an absolute picture, when he opened the coffin lid.

"Please," she begged. "I know it sounds macabre, but he will understand, you'll see."

So, as gently and as carefully as I could, I repeated word for word what Mary Smith had said and finished by saying: "I'm afraid your wife has a very strange sense of humor, Mr. Smith, because she keeps chuckling about the coffin."

To my immense relief, and for the first time since he had walked into my study, Mr. Smith smiled and cried out.

"That's her, that's my Mary, and trust her to think it was funny. Mind you, she's right," he went on, chuckling now himself. "I did have a bloody shock, The hairs on the back of my neck must have stood out a mile, and it's a wonder I didn't turn pure white."

Mary, nodding and smiling herself and agreeing with her husband's comments, then went on to tell me the rest of the story.

She wasn't the only one to die on the coach that day; others also lost their lives. Because of the circumstances, and the fact that the accident had happened abroad, it took several days before the authorities would allow the bodies to be shipped home.

Mr. Smith, along with the other survivors of the crash,

were flown home straightaway, which meant he had been forced to leave the body of his wife behind.

Mary's body, along with the bodies of the other victims, was eventually shipped home to England and delivered on the day of the funeral to Mr. Smith's home. Side by side Mr. Smith and his son stood and watched as the coffin was brought into the house. The grief and sadness that the man and the boy felt drew them close together as both stared at the box that held the body of the woman so dear to them.

Mr. Smith put his arms firmly about his beloved son's shoulders and asked him if he would like to see his mother's face for the last time. The boy, unable to speak, nodded his head, and together they reached forward to lift the coffin lid.

With tears now streaming down their faces, Mary's husband and her child gazed lovingly into the coffin . . . and froze.

For there, lying outstretched and looking for all the world as if in peaceful slumber . . . was a stranger! A total stranger!

Mr. Smith had been given the wrong body.

Mary continued, telling me that her husband, after the initial shock, had simply gone berserk. "He kept repeating, over and over: 'Where's my Mary? What have they done with my Mary?' And all the time," she said, "I was standing by his side, trying desperately to get through to him, to them both. My husband and my son were so distraught, and try as I might, I just could not make them hear me."

Talking of her son, Mary was particularly proud of him and told me that he was hoping to wear a uniform. "Tell Paul that I approve," she said. "It's wonderful news."

At this piece of information Mr. Smith stared, obviously amazed as he exclaimed: "But he only applied a few weeks ago. He's hoping to join the police force."

"Well," I said, "perhaps you could tell your son that his mother knows all about it."

Since that time Mr. Smith has been to see me several times, and the last time was a wonderful occasion for all of us. Mary came through to see me, as usual, and the first thing she said was: "Tell him I think she's lovely. I couldn't have chosen better myself."

Well now, you don't have to be psychic, do you, to understand that message?

Mr. Smith had met someone else, and indeed she was a lovely lady he thought the world of. He was hoping to spend the rest of his life with her, but there was just one snag, one little hurdle he had to get over: he needed his wife's approval. He wanted Mary to tell him, truthfully, what she thought of his new girlfriend.

Mary thought that it was wonderful, and she told me that she felt as if a terrific burden had been lifted from her shoulders.

"I have been so worried about him," she said, "and all I've wanted was for him to find someone to love, and who would love him, too, and look after him properly. Well, now he has," she continued. "It has taken a long time, but he's done it, and I couldn't be more pleased.

"Tell him, will you, please, to be happy, as I am."

So even though Mr. Smith's life had been shattered and in pieces, he has been able, gradually, to pick up those pieces and make a fresh start, a new beginning.

He told me that, but for the evidence given through me of his wife's survival, his life would have been unbearable. That evidence gave him strength.

I was able, he tells me, to help him to see that death, although tragic in Mary's case, is not final. It is not the end, but just a transition from one world to another.

During his first sitting with me, Mr. Smith experienced sadness and laughter mingled together. I know that his memories of his first communication with his wife through a medium will stay with him forever, bringing him strength, comfort, and joy.

The one message from Mary to her husband that stands out clearly in my mind is the one she gave when talking about the mix-up with the coffins.

"I stood by his side," she said, "as he cried out in agony: 'Mary, oh, Mary, where are you?' and I tried my best to make him hear, and to help him to understand.

"I called out to him, and to my son, again and again: 'I'm here, I'm here right next to you.'

"It didn't matter to me," she recalled, "that it was the wrong body. After all, what is a body but an empty shell! I kept on trying to tell them both—I'm not in that coffin, nor am I in any other coffin. The body that I once used is now useless to me, so it doesn't matter what happens to it. All that matters," Mary went on, "is that you, my husband and my son, know how close I am to you.

"I'm right here by your side . . . always!"

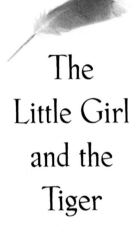

The
Little Girl
and the
Tiger

It began with a phone call, a lady wanting a consultation. "You are a medium, aren't you?" she said quite aggressively, and before I could reply she demanded an appointment for herself and a friend, saying she had lost her daughter and wanted to contact her.

Now, being a medium doesn't automatically mean that I am a nicer or more tolerant person, though I do endeavor to control my thoughts about others. But I'm afraid this phone call niggled me, and something about this woman irritated me a little. So when I had written down her appointment in my diary, by the side I put a question mark, something I usually do if I am unsure about someone.

I then promptly forgot all about it until the week of the sitting, when I looked in my diary and saw the question mark there. At first I couldn't remember why I had written it in, but then it was like hearing her voice all over again as I recalled her telling me that she had lost her daughter.

It is difficult to tell on the telephone what age a person is or what they look like; so I had no idea how old my prospective client would be and therefore had no idea how old her daughter would be. I might be looking for a teenager, a twenty-year-old, or even a forty-year-old. So although I knew my client had lost her daughter, I was still working blind.

The morning of the consultation I woke early. It was about six o'clock, and the first thing that came into my head was, "Oh, no, that woman is coming today." Then, shrugging it off, I turned over, hoping to go back to sleep. As I did so, out of the corner of my eye I saw something move.

Curious, I turned onto my back so that I could have a proper look at whatever it was, and standing before me was a little girl. Visits in this way from those in the spirit world were not at all unusual, but this child was especially cute. She was about four years old and the sweetest, prettiest little thing, with a plump little body, round rosy cheeks, and beautiful blond hair. Her eyes were large and cornflower blue, matching the blue of the dress she wore. Clutched in one hand was a teddy bear, very small, well worn, and ragged looking. What an adorable child, I thought.

Smiling shyly at me, with her free hand she waved. A small child version of a wave, wriggling her chubby little fingers.

"Hello, young lady, what are you doing here?" I asked, smiling gently.

"My mummy's coming to see you today," she whispered.

"Ah," I said, "is she now? And are you going to be a good girl for me, and talk to me when your mummy comes?"

The child nodded and giggled self-consciously, wriggling her little fingers at me all the time, and I smiled at her again and asked: "You will try hard, darling, won't you?"

She bobbed her head up and down, and I took that to mean yes, but when I asked her her name all I got from her was a toothy grin.

I tried again but got nowhere at all, so not wanting to push too hard, I tried another tack: "Is there anything you want me to tell Mummy, or is there anything you want to say to me before your mummy comes this morning?"

Bobbing her head up and down once again, she looked at me with those large cornflower blue eyes and whispered softly, "Tell Mummy 'bout the tiger."

Hopefully, I pursued this and asked: "What about the tiger? Can you tell me about it?" But she merely repeated again:

"Tell my mummy 'bout the tiger." And wriggling her little fingers at me once more, she disappeared as quickly as she had come.

Smiling now and happy, I turned over in bed and cat-napped for another hour before I got up.

My two clients arrived promptly at ten-thirty A.M., and as I showed them into the study, it was obvious to me which one was the lady I had spoken to on the telephone. She had that same demanding tone in her voice. In her early thirties, quite attractive, and with long black hair, she looked nothing like the child I had spoken to earlier.

Her friend was quiet—in fact, quite shy—and she also had blond hair.

Now then, I thought, trying to see some similarities between them and my little visitor, I wonder which one is the mother?

Immediately upon sitting down, I spotted the little girl, who was jumping up and down with excitement, pointing to the darker of the two women, saying: "That's my mummy, it is, it is!"

Using that power, that mind energy, with which I communicate with those in the spirit world and looking to Grey Eagle for confirmation, I began. "All right, darling," I said, laughing, "hold on a minute," and I began to describe the fairy child who was now waiting so patiently.

"That's her, that's her," her mother gasped, "that's my Mandy," and fishing in her handbag, she brought out a photograph, which she handed to me. The photo didn't do justice to the child I had standing before me, but it was obviously the same child.

Smiling encouragement, I said: "All right now, Mandy, what would you like to tell your mummy?"

Pouting and cross with me because she thought I must have forgotten, she admonished: "You haven't told Mummy. You've got to tell Mummy 'bout the tiger."

So I explained to Mandy's mother how her daughter had visited me earlier that morning and that she had asked me to talk about "the tiger."

My client, puzzled by this, shook her head, saying, "I'm sorry, but I don't know what she means."

Going back to Mandy, I asked gently, "Sweetheart, can you tell me a little more about the tiger so that I can help Mummy to understand?"

But all she would say again was: "Tell my Mummy 'bout the tiger."

Now when it comes to dealing with small children, I can have infinite patience, which I needed, as Mandy is a stubborn little girl. Having decided that her mother did know what she was talking about, she refused to reveal any more information, no matter what I said or did. Her mother just became more and more puzzled each time I asked.

"Perhaps Mandy had a toy tiger, or was she perhaps fond of tigers at the zoo?"

Eventually I ran out of ideas, and in desperation I asked Grey Eagle. I should, of course, have asked him sooner.

Chuckling, he said, "It's easy—look." As in a vision, I was shown a cat, a large tom, with ginger and white stripes. It was the sort of cat a small child might mistake for a tiger.

"Tell Mandy's mother what you see," continued my guide, "and then ask if she has seen one this morning, early, at about six-thirty A.M."

When I relayed all of this information to Mandy's mother, I really thought at first that she was going to faint.

Then, slowly, tears began to trickle down her face, and in a voice barely above a whisper, she said: "My Mandy really is alive. She really can see me after all.

"I got up early this morning," she went on, "because I had such a lot to do, what with getting the boys off to school and one thing and another. The milkman had just been when I came down the stairs, so I went out to fetch the milk in. Just as I stepped out of the door a cat shot straight under my feet. It came out of nowhere and I almost went flying. It was a huge thing with ginger and white stripes, and now I come to mention it, Mandy's right . . . it did look just like a little tiger."

Mandy, now very pleased with herself because she had been right and her mummy did, after all, know about the tiger, went on to tell me many more things.

Her favorite topic was her two brothers, both on this side, whom she obviously adored and who, by the sound of things, were real mischiefs. The older of the two was always getting into trouble, and Mandy gleefully related tales of his exploits.

Because she was so young, occasionally I had a little trouble understanding her. One minute she seemed just a baby and the next quite grown-up. But there was no mistaking one statement she made.

She was still talking about her brothers, and as she was describing how they would sit on the floor and draw pictures and swap coloring books, she said: "And they have sweeties, too—and Andrew always has a black mouth—and a black tongue." And then, in a small conspiratorial whisper, "He loves lick-rish, see, it's his favorite."

Mandy's mother laughed at this and confirmed that indeed her youngest son adored licorice.

At this point I hadn't yet discovered how Mandy had passed into the spirit world, and I didn't want to upset the child by asking her. But Grey Eagle, realizing that this information was necessary for Mandy's mother, gave me all the details.

It had happened on a warm summer's day, and Mandy had been playing outside on the path near her house. Her mother had repeatedly warned her not to go on the road, but on this day the temptation was too great.

She heard the familiar tinkling of the ice-cream van as it came round the corner, and in her excitement, she forgot her mother's warning.

"Ice cream," she squealed delightedly, and raced out into the road.

The driver of the car didn't stand a chance of avoiding her, and Mandy was killed instantly.

Mandy's mother confirmed all of this, and now sobbing,

she told me of the guilt and self-recriminations she had had since her daughter's death—and how she had gone from medium to medium in a desperate search for evidence of Mandy's survival.

"I haven't known a moment's peace," she said, "until now, and I have come up against so many blank walls trying to find the truth."

I smiled and asked: "Just what was it that has been said this morning that has finally convinced you that your Mandy has survived death?"

She answered without hesitation and with no more doubts left in her mind: "The tiger."

Such a trivial but oh so significant piece of evidence. But such was the power of this evidence that it brought real peace to Mandy's mother and a true understanding that life really does continue on.

Mandy's mother could now rest easy, knowing that her daughter was indeed alive and safe.

But for me, the most important thing was that Mandy was finally content. She had her family back . . . and they knew it.

Mary

So far, throughout this case book, each story has shown the will and determination of those in the spirit world, of their need and perseverance to communicate. This next story reveals a woman's singleness of purpose as she determines to reach the husband and children she so sadly had to leave.

She came through in a session with a client named Doreen Abrams. Doreen was a familiar face, and this was her third sitting.

Looking to Grey Eagle, as I always do, I began, "I have a lady standing beside me, and although I can't see her very clearly I am having no difficulty whatsoever in hearing her. Her name, she tells me, is Mary, and she has explained that she passed, quite recently, with cancer."

Doreen shook her head. "Oh, no," she said, "I'm afraid it doesn't mean anything at all to me."

But there it was again, very clear and very precise.

"My name is Mary, and I passed with cancer. I'm her

neighbor, Doreen's neighbor. Tell her I've been watching her these last two days going backward and forward, from her house to mine, climbing over the fence."

"But it can't be," said a startled Doreen as I passed on the message. "It can't be *that* Mary, my neighbor Mary, because, well, she only died three days ago. It won't be her, Rosemary, surely. She couldn't do it so quickly . . . could she?"

By "it" Doreen had meant that she didn't think Mary would be able to communicate through a medium so soon. For some strange reason she thought, like many people, that those in the spirit world had to have passed at least six months, if not longer, before being able to form any kind of communication link.

Mary had shown her that this just wasn't so. Some folk take years before they feel ready to make themselves known, usually through a medium, after they have passed. Others manage within hours, and a few, for reasons of their own, just won't do it at all.

Poor Doreen had a hard time at first accepting that her next-door neighbor, whose funeral she was going to the next day, could actually make contact in such a short time. Then bewilderment turned to amazement as Mary continued with her messages.

She mentioned her two daughters—Joanne, who was thirteen years old, and Rachel, ten years old—naturally showing tremendous concern because they were crying so much. At one point I asked Doreen: "Who's Martin? Mary mentions Martin, and whoever he is she loves him dearly."

Martin, I was told by Doreen, was Mary's husband.

"And send my love to Mike, and tell him I'm fine now, will you?" Mary continued.

Mike was Martin's brother, and they were very close.

Several times during this sitting links were made with members of Doreen's own family. Her father and brother both came through quite clearly, but they were interrupted again and again by Mary. She was desperate to let her family know that she had, very definitely, survived death.

Eventually Mary's interruptions became impossible to ignore, and I told Doreen so.

"It's just no good, I don't seem able to quiet her. So would you mind, Doreen, if we give Mary more time?"

Now this might sound, to some of you, a strange thing to ask, but you have to remember that Doreen had come to see me in the hope of getting in touch with *her* family. And here we had her next-door neighbor, who seemed to be taking over the whole show, not allowing anyone else to say more than a few words before chipping in herself.

Doreen, a lovely lady with a kind and generous nature, understood perfectly. "If that were me," she said, "I would be doing just the same. I would want my family to know how I was, and that I had made it over all right."

So from then on Mary had the floor, and she talked constantly about her family, telling me how they were coping with their loss.

"They're not doing very well, and I know that if Doreen would let Martin hear the tape, both he and the family will feel much better."

On every visit to me Doreen has always recorded her sittings, and this time was no exception. But at the suggestion that she should let her neighbor listen to her tape, Doreen shook her head.

"Oh, no, I don't think so, I really don't think I could do that. I don't think I know him well enough for that," she replied.

Not put off by this in the least, Mary continued. Switching away from her family, she told me that before her passing, her husband had done some alterations to the kitchen.

"He put all new cupboards in," she said, "and a new floor as well. It looks beautiful, and I was really pleased when it was finished. But we need a bread bin, tell Martin, will you? It's important. The kitchen won't be properly finished until he gets the bread bin."

After the sitting was over, Doreen and I talked for a little while, and she asked me what I would do about the tape if I were her.

I explained that in my experience, if someone in spirit makes a request such as this, it is not a request made lightly.

"I am sure," I went on, "that Mary would never ask you to do or say anything to her family which might harm or cause them upset in any way. You have to remember, Doreen, that Mary knows Martin very much better than you do. And all I can tell you is that it is important to Mary."

"But," I added, "if you feel that you just don't want to get involved, then you must not allow either Mary or me to influence you in any way."

Doreen left my house that day in a very pensive mood, and her final words to me as she went out of the door were: "I'll have to think about it. I'll listen to the tape when I get home, and then I will decide what to do."

Later that same day Doreen phoned me, very excited and pleased with herself. She explained that after listening to the tape, she sat, debating in her own mind what she should do. Then, suddenly, and for reasons she could not explain, she took her courage in both hands. Grabbing the tape recorder and climbing over the fence, as Mary had described her doing, she knocked on her neighbor's door.

Martin, a tall slim man in his late thirties, smiled a welcome as he let Doreen in and showed her through to the sitting room. She sat on the edge of the chair that Martin had offered, wondering where to begin, what to say first. When she noticed Martin's curious glances toward her tape recorder, she took a deep breath and began.

"I suppose, Martin, you must be wondering why I've come, and what I've brought the tape recorder for. Well, you see, it's like this," and she gave him Mary's messages, suggesting that he should hear the tape.

His face completely expressionless, Martin nodded his agreement. "I don't suppose," he said, "that there can be any harm in listening, can there?"

Doreen shakily set up the machine, but just as she was about to switch it on, in walked Martin's brother, Mike.

Martin explained briefly to Mike what was happening and asked him to stay and listen.

For the next hour the two brothers sat with Doreen, quite still and not saying a word. The only sound in the room was the voice of a stranger talking of things that not even friends of Martin's family knew.

Every so often Doreen would glance furtively across at the two men, hoping for some indication of their reaction to what they were hearing. But both sat perfectly still, their faces giving away nothing at all.

Then came Mary's last message, conveyed, of course, through me:

"Please, Doreen, give my love to Martin and the girls. Tell them I'm all right, and that I have survived."

The tape ended, and for the next few minutes the two men sat, still not saying a word. Doreen, now feeling very embarrassed by their silence, picked up the tape recorder and made to leave.

It was as she stood up to go that Martin seemed suddenly to come to life. Jumping out of his chair, he moved across to where Doreen stood, and putting his arm around her, he gently pushed her back onto the chair.

"I don't know what to say," he began, "or how to thank you for what you have just given me." And words of thanks and gratitude tumbled from him.

He told Doreen that he had understood all of what he had heard, even about the bread bin. It was the one thing left to buy to complete the set of kitchen equipment that Mary had been collecting. It was also one of the last things that Mary had mentioned to her husband before she had "died."

He then told Doreen that he had been so depressed before he heard the tape, and he had been wondering how on earth he would be able to face Mary's funeral and how he would ever manage to be strong for his children's sake.

"You know, Doreen, Mary believed in a life after death, and we talked about it many times. She promised me, just before she 'died,' that if there was a way to send a message to me, to let me know that she was all right, then she would do so. And I believed her. I just didn't expect to hear from her so soon. It's really wonderful, and now I know that I will be able to face tomorrow, knowing that my darling wife is not lost to me or to my girls."

A few days after Mary's funeral, Doreen received a visit from Martin's brother's wife, Val, who had listened to a copy of Doreen's tape.

She made some tea, and the two women chatted for a while, discussing the impact the tape had made on all the family.

"You have no idea how much better we all felt," said Val, "and how much easier it was to cope with Mary's passing. Mind you"—she then chuckled—"it must have seemed a little strange to all those people who came to the funeral.

"They must have thought it very odd, and on such a sad and solemn occasion, that the whole family, especially Martin, were all smiling."

Louise

Like Mary's story, the story of Louise shows the need, not only of her parents, but of her own need to make that communication link which proves survival after death.

It began with a knock on the door, and then I heard Samantha's voice.

"Come in," she said. "Mum won't be long."

Oh, crumbs, I thought. Are they early, or am I late?

I looked at the clock that stood by the bed and realized to my horror that I had been on the phone, on and off, for over two hours.

It had been one of those mornings when, no matter how hard I tried, I simply couldn't get organized. People had been ringing nonstop, one after the other, wanting appointments, advice, healing or absent healing, and, of course, I had to give them my full attention. Not an easy thing to do when I was also trying to get ready for work.

As I raced around the bedroom, finding shoes and brushing my hair at the same time, it occurred to me that I hadn't given much thought to the two people who were downstairs in my study, waiting for me.

Some of you will suppose that a medium must be calm, peaceful, and full of meditative thoughts, especially just before a sitting. Now, while I would agree that it's not a bad suggestion, I'm afraid that for me it simply doesn't work that way. I am usually in a rush and trying desperately to fit everything into my day, which invariably ends up being a day too short.

So as I scrambled furiously under the bed, looking for my missing shoe, I didn't have time to reflect on the circumstances that had led to my working on my one day off in weeks.

I knew that Grey Eagle had felt it important enough to ask me to see these people, and that was good enough for me.

When the gentleman had rung and made the appointment, he had refused to give me any surname. "Just put down John and Sue," he had said.

Eventually, having found the missing shoe, I dashed out of the bedroom—and nearly jumped out of my skin as I was confronted by a young girl of about fourteen years of age.

Recovering quickly, I chuckled and said, "Oh, my, you did give me a fright."

She grinned sheepishly, then gave me a mock curtsy and dashed off in front of me down the stairs. By the time I walked into the study, she was already there, waiting patiently for me to begin.

The couple already seated in the study were in their early

thirties, very ordinary looking, but both seemed very nervous, the young woman more so than her husband.

Explanations, I felt, were not necessary with these two. I had no need to talk about mediumship or to explain in any way what I was going to try to do. They had come to me for one reason and one reason only, and if I did not fill their expectation, they would, I realized, keep on trying until they found somebody who did.

So without any preamble, and much to the delight of the young girl I had nearly bumped into on the landing, I began.

"I have a young girl here, about fourteen years old at a guess, wearing glasses. She tells me she passed due to an accident and says that you are her mum and dad."

The couple nodded, and the young woman bit hard on her lip, but neither of them spoke a word.

Realizing that this couple had decided to say as little as possible to me, in order not to give anything away, I turned back to the young girl, whose name I discovered later was Louise. Communicating my thoughts to her, I said, "Well, sweetheart, it's all up to you. Try, if you can, to tell me as much about yourself and your family as possible."

Quite unperturbed, she replied: "Tell my dad that I know he's hurt his finger."

Such a little thing, and yet so important! With no hesitation I gave the message, but John's reaction was not at all what I expected.

"I haven't hurt my finger at all," he said.

For the next five minutes we argued, his daughter insisting that he had hurt his finger and he equally insistent that he had not. I was sure that he was not being deliberately obstructive, but I was equally sure that Louise knew what she was talking about.

"Look," I said eventually, "I don't want to seem rude, and I can only repeat what I am being told, but your daughter is now describing to me how you stood at the kitchen sink yesterday, with your finger all bloody, and she keeps on saying that you made it bleed."

John looked down at his hands, then across at me, a bewildered look on his face.

There were no scars that I could see, no plasters, no visible signs of injury, but I knew that I was right, that this young girl who had come through from the spirit world was right.

Then Sue spoke up. "She's right, John, Louise is talking about your sore thumb, not your finger."

Understanding dawned, and John then told me how, after his daughter's accident, his nerves completely on edge, he had begun to pick at his thumb, pulling away at the skin and making it bleed.

"It keeps forming a scab," he told me, "and I've tried to stop doing it, but yesterday I forgot, and picked at it again. There was blood everywhere, and I had to put it under the tap and run cold water on it for ages before the bleeding stopped. But how," he went on now, truly perplexed, "could you have possibly known about it?"

I smiled and said gently, "Because, John, your daughter has told me. Now, shall we see if we can all relax a little and see what else Louise would like to say?"

"I was on my bike," Louise said, "doing my paper round, when a car came up fast behind me and knocked me off. He couldn't stop at first," she went on, "and I was dragged down the street. When Mum came to the hospital she was really upset because it didn't look like me anymore."

I carefully related this last piece of information, not

wanting to cause too much distress to Louise's parents but knowing that the more evidence I was able to give, the more they might realize how very much alive their daughter still was.

A tragedy like this is always difficult to relate and is always distressing no matter how carefully it is approached.

One of the hardest aspects of working as a medium is seeing, and sometimes being a part of, the intense pain that parents have to go through when losing a child. It doesn't matter how young or old that child is; whether it is a baby or an adult, it makes no difference. The pain and hurt are always there.

Louise had thought it best to explain, in as much detail as possible, how she had passed over, knowing that her parents would not be satisfied unless they had that evidence.

So we got the worst part over, and then she told me all about her mum and dad, then about her bedroom, her friends, a little bit about her school, and all sorts of other things.

At one point, describing her bedroom, Louise mentioned the pictures that hung on the walls. "She tells me that the pictures are of Michael," I related to John and Sue.

"Oh, no, you're wrong there," said John. "We don't have any pictures of Michael. We don't know any Michael."

But Louise insisted. "Tell them it's George Michael," she said, "my hero."

So again I recounted to John and Sue the information Louise was so sure about, and I added: "Your daughter definitely seems to know what she is talking about, and I for one don't doubt for a minute that she's right."

This remark produced a quiver of a smile from Sue, and John exclaimed, "She's right, the pictures on her bedroom wall are all of Wham, the pop group. You know, George Michael from Wham!"

Louise talked of many more things, gave more evidence of her survival after death, then eventually started talking about her sister, Lisa, who is still on this side.

Lisa is handicapped and goes to a special school. Although she is not physically disabled, her parents have had many many problems with Lisa, the worst being that she is an extremely hyperactive child. Even getting her to bed, or to sleep at all, was virtually impossible sometimes.

John and Sue had been to numerous doctors and specialists and had been given a number of different drugs to try, in order to help Lisa to settle down. They wanted desperately to see their daughter leading as normal a life as possible, but nothing they had tried had helped.

"We're at our wits' end," they said, and John confessed that he would give anything to help Lisa.

"We know that she will never be able to live a completely normal life, but surely something could be done to help her," he said. "We have been all over and tried everything, but it just seems as if we're banging our heads against a brick wall."

Surely, I thought, there must be something we could do to help.

I looked at Louise, who, having read my thoughts, smiled sweetly and said: "Don't worry, he's going to help." And she pointed to where my friend and guide was standing.

Grey Eagle nodded, then, leaning forward toward Louise and in a conspiratorial manner, he whispered something in her ear.

She grinned delightedly, then: "It's her diet, 'he' says it's her diet. Lisa is eating things which make her poorly. 'He' says, Grey Eagle, I mean, that I've got to tell you it's her diet!"

I looked at this young girl, who was so eager to help her sister, and I marveled at her ability to accept so easily the fact that Grey Eagle knew what he was talking about. But I knew that it would not be so easy to convince her parents to listen.

Even I, though not questioning the wisdom of my guide, thought that it really did sound a little too simple.

When I told John and Sue what Grey Eagle and Louise had said, they both looked at me as if I had gone mad.

"Believe me," I said, "I know what you must be thinking, and I am aware that what I have said might, to you, sound preposterous, but my guide does know what he's talking about. If he insists, as he does, that some of the food which Lisa eats is causing her to be hyperactive, then my advice is that you try and get her to have some allergy tests done, to see if she is allergic to anything she is eating."

Mainly because Louise had been able to provide them with so much evidence of her survival, John and Sue listened to our diagnosis of Lisa's problem and later talked over all that had been said. The evidence they had been given that had brought them together again with the daughter they had lost so tragically now helped them take a major step toward helping the daughter who was still with them on this side.

John rang a homeopathist whose name I had given and, explaining Lisa's problem, asked if it would be possible to have some tests carried out. Unable to help, the homeopathist suggested that John get in touch with a doctor in Manchester, a Dr. Mumby, who specializes in allergies. This they did.

Dr. Mumby asked first for a list of all the foods Lisa normally ate, so that he could begin by testing Lisa's reactions to those foods.

The result of all those tests was that poor Lisa is allergic to just about everything that she had been eating. Pork and corn were two of the worst offenders, but it was discovered that Lisa's system reacted adversely to many other foods as well.

With much perseverance, a suitable diet was found, and although it isn't always easy for John and Sue to keep Lisa to it, they are determined to try.

Approximately three months after Lisa was put onto this new diet, there was a distinct improvement in her behavior. After six months even the staff at Lisa's school were admitting a marked difference.

No longer was Lisa uncontrollably hyperactive, and she is happier and much more contented. Sue tells me that it was wonderful actually to be able to put her daughter to bed at eight o'clock P.M. and know that she would sleep until eight the next morning. So not only did Lisa benefit, but her parents did also.

John and Sue Harrison have battled against extreme difficulties in order to help their daughter Lisa, and they are, without doubt, winning that battle.

The battle they face in coming to terms over the tragic loss of their daughter Louise is still being fought. Whether or not they win or lose that battle remains to be seen, but one thing, I know, is certain. Louise will do all she can to help her parents, as she did indeed to help her sister, Lisa.

The
Scientist

Our case book ends with this last story, which tells how, once again, those in the spirit world can give us specific and constructive help. Like John and Sue Harrison and so many others, Kathryn and Christian Langton were shown a clear path . . . a path they chose to follow.

I first met Kathryn Langton, a nurse who works at the Doncaster Royal Infirmary in the north of England, when she and her mother came to me for a consultation. The main purpose for their visit was to make a communication link with Kathryn's father. He had passed very suddenly and without warning, with a massive heart attack, as he informed me when we managed to form the link.

Kathryn was delighted, thrilled to hear from her father. She was also surprised and pleased when I discovered, through Grey Eagle, that she possessed the gift of healing.

She began classes with me to develop her gift, and it was during one class that Kathryn received yet another message from my guide. But this time the message was not for her, but for her husband, Christian Langton. It was a small yet significant piece of information concerning a lost member of his family, and he had to do a little investigating before he discovered that this lady did indeed exist.

Being very stubborn, and not wanting to give up years of scientific thinking, Christian was reluctant to come to me for a sitting. Yet he felt he needed to talk to me. So I was invited to the Langtons' house for tea.

After being bombarded with dozens of questions, some that I could answer, many I couldn't, my host was more confused than ever. His thinking was black and white; mine varied shades and colors. His questions were based on scientific law; my answers were based on knowledge, through experience, of another dimension to life. He was getting nowhere.

Help eventually came in the form of Christian's grandfather, who, having passed to the spirit world some years earlier, had been awaiting his opportunity.

It was fascinating for me, and astounding for Christian, to witness the barriers of science, the barriers that separate our two worlds, slowly disintegrate. The evidence of another world, another life, mounted increasingly, until it would have been ridiculous, even for a stubborn scientist, to dismiss the evidence of his own ears. The evidence of a life after death.

But it didn't stop there.

It was not enough for Christian's grandfather to prove his existence after death. He also wanted to show his grandson that he could still be involved in the things that went on in this world and that he could help with problems if allowed.

Christian Langton is a research scientist and was, at the time of this impromptu sitting, working on a project involving bone analysis. He had designed and built a machine, called an Ultrasonic Bone Analyzer, which is able to detect osteoporosis. Osteoporosis is a disease that results from loss of estrogen at menopause, causing fracture of the hip, spine, and wrist, and affects one in four women. By using Christian's machine, doctors could detect and treat this condition before it became a problem.

The idea of measuring bone, using the ankle bone, with ultrasonic sound waves, was a good one, and Christian knew it could work. But his machine, which when his grandfather described it looked to me like a goldfish tank, was still at the testing stage, and there were problems. All the tests so far had failed to produce consistent satisfactory results. After much consideration and many sleepless nights, Christian became convinced that the only thing that could be wrong was the angle of the footrest inside the tank.

Now I've mentioned that the machine looked to me like a goldfish tank, clear Perspex, half filled with water.

Naturally, as I described this thing to Christian, his interest sharpened, and amazement showed on his face as I informed him that his grandfather knew of the difficulties he was having.

"Well," he replied dryly, "perhaps the old boy would be good enough to help me solve them." Of course, in saying this, Christian didn't really expect that his grandfather would really oblige.

But he did.

"Tell him"—he chuckled delightedly—"that he's barking up the wrong tree. The angle of the footrest is fine, it's the water that's the problem." And he went on to explain how to put it right. Talking in technical terms I didn't understand, but Christian did, he basically said by removing the water and placing the ultrasonic transducers directly against the skin, the problem would be solved. Christian, hearing this, wondered what he was going to say to his colleagues in explanation of the new changes to his project. How could he show them, in a scientific way, that he had reached these conclusions? . . . Could he simply say, "Well, you see, my grandfather told me."

Less than a week later, Christian Langton had corrected the faults on his Ultrasonic Bone Analyzer, following his grandfather's instructions to the letter, and you can now find these machines being used in hospitals in Europe, Australia, Canada, Japan and many other countries throughout the world.

It is often pointed out, by those who know no better, that the information mediums supply through spirit is trivial and useless. Christian Langton, a scientist of international renown, a very astute and free-thinking man, would, I know, disagree. And so, wholeheartedly, would I.

It may well be that with time Christian could have solved his problems his own way. But as a medium I feel great satisfaction in knowing that I was used as the instrument that brought together our scientific world and the spirit world, for the greater good of humankind. I know that this is an area that has as yet remained basically untapped, but I feel certain that as more and more people become aware of the scope and range of information that mediums can connect into, and as confidence in spirit communication grows, which it will, then the link between manmade science and natural science and scientists will, in turn, grow ever stronger.

PART IV

*The
Power
Expanded*

Healing

So much water had gone under the bridge. My life was now so changed. No longer afraid. No longer timid and shy. My life was more stable, more secure. Grey Eagle had taught me many things, my confidence had grown . . . and I was growing stronger.

I had come to Cyprus with my daughter, Samantha, and my boyfriend at that time, and it was the first holiday we had all been on together. The year was 1983.

We had saved like mad and had rented a comfortable three-bedroom flat for four weeks. Four weeks of glorious sunshine, wonderful Greek food, my favorite, and rest, lots and lots of rest.

We had spent the day on the beach, just lazing around, swimming in the sea, and watching some Greek divers catching octopus.

Driving home, we decided to stop at one of the many restaurants dotted along the roadside and get something to eat. Sitting in the shade of the olive trees with a long cold drink in my hand, I gazed around at the small tables with their brightly colored umbrellas and admired the lovely tropical plants in the gardens.

The sky was blue and cloudless, the air fresh and clean. For the first time in over three years I was truly relaxed. Not worrying, not working, not even thinking. Just sipping my drink and waiting patiently for my dinner, and if the tantalizing smell coming from the direction of the restaurant was anything to go by, the food was going to taste delicious.

King prawns in a mild garlic sauce, followed by lamb kebabs, Greek salad, and some home-baked crusty bread. And to finish, a huge bowl of strawberries piled high with fresh cream. Gorgeous! Now a good brandy would be an ideal way to finish this excellent meal.

We paid the bill and were just about to leave when the waitress approached our table. Pulling out a chair, she unceremoniously plonked herself down.

"Ah, that's better"—she sighed—"I can rest for a while, until the next rush, that is." And she began chatting with us. She talked about how she and her husband had come over from America and set up in business. Then, looking at me, she asked, "Do you work?"

Quietly I answered: "Yes, I'm a medium."

"Well!" she exclaimed. "How interesting, and what a coincidence that we have met. You see, a good friend of mine, who lives in a small village not far from here, is a healer."

I was immediately interested and began asking all sorts of questions. What was his name? What did he do for a living? And where did he live?

His name, our waitress told us, was John Mikaledes, he

lived in the small village of Spitali, and he earned his living as a water diviner.

This last piece of information intrigued me more than ever, and I asked, "Do you think it would be possible for us to meet this man?"

Our newfound friend smiled and assured us that all we needed to do was to find his village. "Anyone who lives there will know him," she said, "and providing you find him at home, he will, I'm sure, be delighted to see you."

She drew us a map and explained how we could get to Spitali, a tiny place in the foothills of the Troodos mountains.

It seemed an easy enough place to got to, even though on the map the roads did look a bit narrow. It was also quite far away, which reminded us of an important detail. What if, after traveling for miles through seemingly barren country, the gentleman we were seeking wasn't at home? Would we have wasted a journey?

But I had got the bit between my teeth, so the following Sunday we set off on our search.

As we drove it seemed that we were slowly leaving civilization behind us, and we went farther and farther into the back of beyond.

After driving for miles and miles on a hot and dusty road, we finally came to a sign that read "Spitali Village." We drove slowly down the deserted main street—or should I say, more correctly, the only street—looking for signs of life.

Suddenly the road widened, and we found ourselves in the small village square, which was also deserted . . . except, that is, for a solitary figure. A tall slim man, standing alone in the middle of the square, waiting, it seemed. But for what? Surely no buses or any public transport came through this tiny place.

He didn't move as the car approached him, and I expected Gordon to stop, but instead we drove straight past him. Then I heard myself say, "That's him. That's the man we're looking for. That man is John Mikaledes."

For a second or two Gordon looked at me as if he thought the heat had gone to my head. "Don't be silly," he scoffed. "He's not standing there waiting for us to arrive when he didn't even know we were coming."

But even as he was saying this, he realized that I was right, so he turned the car around and back into the square we went.

The man we had passed only moments before was still there, waiting.

Gordon pulled the car up alongside him, and leaning out of the window, he said very tentatively: "We are looking for a man by the name of John Mikaledes."

The man leaned toward the car, and looking past Gordon straight at me, he smiled and in perfect English replied: "I am he, I am John Mikaledes, and I think I must be waiting for you," and, turning on his heel, he said, "Follow me."

He led us to a small white bungalow that stood on the outskirts of the village on top of a cliff. The view was magnificent and the air pure and clean. It was heaven to get out of the car, stretch our legs, and take in the picture of this beautiful little paradise set in the middle of nowhere.

A small plump lady in her mid-fifties came bustling out of the house to welcome us, and before we knew it we were sitting in a neat little room, drinking freshly squeezed orange juice, ice cold and delicious, and helping ourselves to juicy-looking chunks of watermelon that Maria, John's wife, had placed on the coffee table in front of us.

When we were well and truly settled, with John and Maria Mikaledes sitting opposite us, John asked, "How did you come to be here, and how or what can I do to help you?" Chuckling, he then added, "Perhaps you could also explain how it was that I have walked four miles to work today, and when I got there I heard a voice insisting that I must come home again, and stand and wait in the village square."

He continued telling us that he had been water divining that morning on a piece of land that was, hopefully, to become building land.

"I do it all the time," he said, "and if I find water, which I often do, I get paid."

He went on, telling us how, with his divining rods, he had been looking in a specific area, when suddenly he heard a voice.

"Go back to Spitali. Go back home. Go back now."

At first his reaction was to ignore the voice because he felt he was close to discovering the water he had walked all the way to find. But then the voice came again, more insistent than ever: "Go back to Spitali. Go home and wait."

So, putting his rods back in his work bag, he turned and walked the four miles back to his village and eventually found himself standing, a little bemused, in the middle of the village square. And just as he had begun to wonder what on earth he was doing, coming home at that hour of the day with no work done and apparently for no reason, he saw our car approach, and he heard a stranger's voice asking: "How can we find John Mikaledes?"

We had a wonderful afternoon with John and Maria. They told us how they had met and married in England after the war, and John told us how he had become involved with the spiritualist church. It was then that he'd discovered that he was a natural healer and begun to practice his healing gifts.

"But do you know, Rosemary," he said, "although I was an active member of the church for years and did a great deal as a healer, maybe there was one message from a medium that was at all relevant to me?"

I then explained to John and Maria that I was a medium, and I asked John if he would like a consultation with me.

Maria laughed and said: "That's just what he's been hoping you would say." So the two of us went into the kitchen, while Maria took Samantha and Gordon on a tour of their small estate.

I began the sitting, finding it easy and relaxed, and my newfound colleague sat, tears streaming down his face, as I gave him first one message, then another, and another. All from the one person he had been waiting to hear from for over twenty years—his mother.

She told John, through me, of her excitement when John became involved with the spiritualist movement in England and became a healer. "Tell him I work with him, giving my energy, sending my love and inspiration," she said.

Then Grey Eagle spoke, giving John one final message, the most important of all.

The reason for my meeting with John Mikaledes was revealed, and all became clear.

Since going back home to Cyprus ten years earlier, John had had many disappointments concerning his spiritual work. Although at first he had tried to continue with his healing, it had become more and more difficult as time went on. Lack of interest and lack of opportunity had finally forced him to give up, so he had left his healing behind.

"The time has come," said Grey Eagle through me, "to begin your healing work again, for you have been too long away from it. It is important, not only for you, but also for the people around you, that your spiritual work should now continue."

John shrugged his shoulders and shook his head in despair. "But where do I begin?" he answered.

"I really don't know," I replied, and added with absolute confidence, "but before I leave Cyprus you will have begun your healing work again."

We left the village of Spitali, having arranged to go back for another visit before our holiday was over, and arrived back at the flat, tired, hungry, and thirsty, but pleased with the day.

I made sandwiches and drinks, and we went out onto the terrace to eat. When the last crumb was gone, we were just about to turn in when a knock came at the door.

Now the last thing you expect when you're on holiday abroad is visitors at ten o'clock at night. The owner of the block of flats we were in had taken it into her head to pay us a visit to make sure that we had settled in and had no complaints.

Of course we offered her a drink, which she accepted, and for the next two hours she stayed and talked.

Her name was Rebecca, and she and her family, two daughters and a son, owned and rented out property and also owned a vineyard and a travel company, which they ran together as a family.

Rebecca was a rather forceful and forthright lady, but I liked her from the first. As soon as she discovered that I was a medium, she was immediately interested, and pretty soon we were telling her all about our meeting with John and Maria Mikaledes. At first she found it difficult to believe that there was such a man in her own country, and virtually on her own doorstep, whom she hadn't heard of. Then she began asking all sorts of questions about him.

"Don't think that I am being nosy, please," she said. "There is a very good reason for my curiosity. You see, my youngest daughter has a problem with her spine. It has begun to curve quite badly, and the specialist is afraid that she may, in time, become crippled.

"I wonder," she continued, "if it would be worth her while going to see this man." And she asked, "Do you think it would do any good?"

"It can't hurt to try," I said, "but it has to be your daughter's decision. Why don't you ask her and see what she says?"

The next morning early, the phone rang. It was Rebecca, asking if we would like to join her and her family for breakfast.

"I've had a word with my daughter," she said, "and she can't wait to meet you all. She is also very keen to meet your healer friend, and to try some healing."

We agreed to take her the next day to see him, and although we didn't have as unusual a reception as we'd had on our first visit, John and Maria were at home, and they were delighted to see us again.

I introduced Rebecca and her daughter and explained the reason for our visit.

John took over immediately. Reaching out for the young girl's hand, he invited her into the house.

Now it was my turn to be shown, with my family, around the garden of John and Maria's small house.

I knew that John would be giving healing, and I prayed silently that he would be able to help.

Twice more we visited John and Maria before we came back to England, and each time we took Rebecca's daughter with us for healing. It was amazing how well she responded to John and how receptive she was to the healing he gave her.

Good healers are not easy to find, but my friend and mentor, Grey Eagle, had indeed been instrumental in guiding me to one who was a rare and special breed. A man of uncommon humility, devotion to spirit, and willingness to give to others, without favor, his love.

The following Christmas we received a card and a letter from John and Maria Mikaledes.

Rebecca's daughter, they said, was still coming for healing and improving slowly. Rebecca had also been given healing regularly, and so had the rest of the family.

But the most remarkable thing was that, due initially to Rebecca, the word about John had spread, and many more people had begun to seek healing.

Maria wrote: "John and I have been simply amazed at the response we have had, and whether he likes it or not, he has his hands full. Every day new people come to us wanting healing, and, of course, he never refuses."

So, now, once again, John Mikaledes is a full-time healer.

This experience, and many others, has taught me that there is no such thing as coincidence, that our often "chance" meetings are planned. Planned by a greater, a universal force, which we here on earth have so little knowledge of.

The ways and workings of the universe are, indeed, wondrous!

Rosemary
the
Healer

John Mikaledes was a fine healer. He had decided to go into this work knowing that it was what he wanted to do.

But it was never my intention to become a healer. For one thing, after my own experiences with doctors, hospitals, and sickness, having had kidney problems in my early twenties, becoming involved with that constant round of pain, despair, and fear was the last thing I wanted to do. Second, I really felt that I did not have what it takes to give healing in the way that I saw Paul Denham and Mick McGuire do. These two men were dedicated, strong, and able to deal with people's needs in a way that I felt in the beginning unable to do. Other people's illnesses reminded me of my own vulnerability, my own weaknesses, and of course my own fear, and I was not ready to be reminded in any way of my human frailties. Let that knowledge sit somewhere in the deep recesses of my subconscious mind. I was happier that way . . . much happier.

In the beginning, the responsibilities of a healer were something I felt unable to deal with, but Grey Eagle was with me, and as my confidence grew I learned gradually to accept my role as a healer as well as that of a medium.

I discovered that healing, the gift of healing, was not a separate thing, but an extension of my mediumship, and my guide encouraged me and carefully steered me as he taught me to discover and use the energy, healing energy, I had been born with.

I had watched Mick McGuire often with his patients, had seen the way they had looked at him, looked to him, for strength and for hope. He always knew instinctively the right things to say, the right way to handle any given situation. He would usually begin by placing his hands on the patient's head or shoulders, tuning in to that great source of healing energy, God energy, which is of the universe. Drawing it to him, combining it with his own energy, he would then endeavor by sheer will to direct that energy toward his patient.

I once saw him with a young woman, a patient of his who was severely crippled with multiple sclerosis. Not only was she struggling with this dreadful and debilitating disease, but she also had the added stress of coping with the fact that her husband had just left her for another woman. Mick was wonderful with her. He promised no miracle cures, no magic wand, no knight in shining armor come to save her. He had listened to her story, and when she had finished he'd held out his arms to her and given her comfort in the knowledge that someone cared, that he cared. When she was calmer and the tears had subsided, he talked to her about his gift, the gift of healing, of the laying on of hands as Christ had once done. Then, quietly and gently, and with no fanfare, no hocus-pocus, he proceeded to give her healing.

As I watched, I saw her visibly relax. Slowly, as she unwound, I was aware of a letting go, subtle as it was, and I knew that she was releasing a little of the hurt, of the loneliness and the fear. Of course this would be a slow process, it would take several sessions with Mick before she would feel totally at ease, I knew that, but I also knew that I was witness to the beginning of that process. I was witness to that feeling in her of safety and trust for a man who held her hand and gave his love in a way no one had given to her before.

There are many who would suppose that to give healing is to attempt to cure a physical ailment, which of course it is. But first and foremost, healing is given to the spirit of the patient, the spirit self, which is the light of the soul. We try to give energy and power to feed that light to make it brighter.

Mick gave his energy. He gave his love, and when I talk of love in this way, I talk of the love that God inspires, that God force that is deep within us, which some recognize and grow from. Many races, many creeds, will have a different name for it, but call it God or Allah or any other name, it does not make a difference. What we are talking of here is that universal force, that great power that is goodness and that, if used wisely, will bring about peace, harmony, and that word again . . . love.

As I progressed with my work, my mediumship, I began giving spiritual self-awareness classes every Friday evening. More and more people were coming to me wanting to learn about the psychic world, and I felt that perhaps I could help in this way, maybe teach them to grow in their understanding of themselves and of their spiritual selves, of the light within them.

Grey Eagle was with me all the way, of course, giving his help and guidance not just to me, but through me to my students. He would give words of encouragement and instruction as to how we could become more sensitive to that universal energy we so wanted and needed to tap into. Looking back, I now realize he was waiting for the inevitable. Curiously (although of course not curiously at all), it seemed that the more I worked as a medium and a teacher, the more those students who came seeking knowledge were those with a special interest and a special talent for healing. You do not have to be psychic to be a healer and I found my classroom sessions became centered on the art of healing (which I explain more about later in this chapter) and for the need of healers to have a careful and thorough training program. Not surprising, then, I found myself, with Grey Eagle's help, involved in a method of training that went deeper and was more thorough than any training program I had come across before that time—or have experienced since. I cannot, nor will I, enlarge upon this further in this book, as to do so would be to ignore the responsibilities of the teacher/student relationship, and this would be a case of a little knowledge being a dangerous thing.

It was some time later, maybe three years later, that I heard myself say to one particular class, "Now is the time for us to go forth into the world and share with others the knowledge we have gained. To share with others the gift of healing."

Shocked, nervous, unsure of their abilities, my students panicked for a while. The thought of opening up a healing center, even though this meant renting a room or hall for just one night a week, with all its implications, responsibility, success or lack of it, dealing with real people with real illnesses . . . it seemed too much for them, and they voiced their fears loudly.

Unbeknownst to them, I was just as surprised. I had heard Grey Eagle's words, had spoken them—"Go out, now is the time"—but he had given me no prior warning of this. So, a little stunned, myself, I listened as my students came up with first one reason, then another, as to why we should not go ahead with this plan. But then, as the realization of what this meant began to sink in, and the task ahead became more apparent to me, I knew that this was something we had to do and soon.

Gently but firmly I talked with my class, helping them to understand that this was not something we would be doing alone, that we would be given help and inspiration, strength to do whatever it was that we must do, and guidance to do our work in the way that God intended we should. We would be given help, as much help as we might need from those in the spirit world and from Grey Eagle. We were just a handful of people, with no real idea or framework, no plan to follow—working in the dark, with only the light of those in the spirit world to guide us . . . and our faith.

Just two weeks later our first healing center was opened. That was in August of 1985. By 1993 we had opened our seventh center, had become a bona fide healing organization allied to the British Alliance of Healing Association and the Confederation of Healing Organizations and on the *British National Register.* We are a charitable organization, and not one of our team is paid for the healing work we do. None of us is wealthy, and the majority of the team, which includes nurses, office workers, professional artists, shopkeepers, and the like, have to work to earn a living. I am no exception, and of course, as a medium, I take private consultations for which I charge, and this is my living. If it were not for this, I, like my team, would not be able to dedicate so much of my time to our organization. There are periods when I spend more time in my capacity as a healer than in that of a medium, going out to homes and hospitals, visiting patients who are unable to attend the centers. Helping to run and organize an association such as ours, even though it is small, can take up a vast amount of time and energy. Many people around the world have come to us for healing when all else fails—young and old, believing and unbelieving, and with a variety of illnesses and problems, some physical, some emotional.

Caroline was just seven years old and crippled. She had not been able to straighten her right leg since she was two years old. Her parents were desperate. Caroline's leg from the knee down was becoming thinner, and the doctors feared that her leg muscles were wasting. There had been some talk of possible amputation of part of the leg if the muscles continued to waste away. No one knew the cause of the problem. Numerous tests and operations had shown very little to explain the situation, the doctors were baffled, not knowing how to proceed further. It was the talk of amputation that spurred Caroline's parents to visit one of our centers, although they were very nervous and highly skeptical. A neighbor, a patient of ours, had told them about us, and they had decided that at this point anything was worth a try.

Caroline was our patient for about eighteen months, coming each week, always a bunch of blue ribbons pinned to her dress (my gift to her). Sometimes she would be tearful, occasionally reticent, but mostly she was willing to have me coax a smile from her. Eventually trusting, she grew in confidence and in determination.

Our team of healers and student healers, under my guidance, worked steadily and with dedication, using our energy, connecting with that universal energy, centering ourselves so that we were good channels for that healing energy to pass through, marveling as each week a little more progress was made. Still, of course, Caroline saw her doctors regularly—we always advise our patients to do this—and they too marveled at her sudden and steady progress. Then eventually, after several months, one evening she walked into the healing center, not hopping as she usually did, but with both feet firmly down, her head held high, and her eyes on my face, waiting for my reaction. Finally, after many months of uncertainty and hard work, we knew that she had made it.

Now she is a healthy, normal little girl, very active with her swimming and her bike riding. Her legs are strong, the muscles developing as they should, and she and her family are at peace.

The last time I spoke with Caroline's father, he told me, "Rosemary, I'm not sure if the healing you gave Caroline made any difference as far as healing in a physical sense. Did it actually change the structure of her leg so that she could straighten it, I don't know. But one thing I do know that made the difference in my daughter's healing process. You gave her the will to believe in herself; somehow you gave her the strength to try. The way she thinks, her attitude, has changed so much and in such a positive way. She trusts now, not just in you, but more importantly she trusts in herself and in her ability to live a normal and fulfilling life. I will never be able to thank you enough."

It is at these times when my team and I feel the real rewards for our efforts, when we know why we work so hard and feel so dedicated, when we can smile and quietly say, "Thank God for the gift to heal."

How can I explain how healing works? When I talk of energy, universal . . . God . . . energy, that healing energy which a healer can "plug" into in the same way we might use electricity, I liken it to that same electric power, unseen and intangible, but nevertheless just as real and much more powerful. A healer will, using mind . . . thought . . . energy, project a thought out to the universe. The universe receives this thought, this pulse of energy, and combines its energy, which is then transmitted back to the healer and then on through to the patient. As far as the patient and the healer are concerned, this is, even though so powerful, still a gentle art. The patient will either sit or lie in a comfortable position in order to relax, and the healer will at first place his/her hands upon the patient, sometimes on the patient's shoulders, sometimes on the patient's head. Then, becoming very still, the healer will listen as his senses tell him where his healing energy is needed most. If a patient has breathing problems, then obviously the healer will "feel" directed to place her hands on the patient's chest. Likewise if the patient has a leg injury, the healer will most likely place his/her hands on the affected area, although not necessarily. No dramatics, no strange antics. The patient will inevitably relax, often going into a gentle sleep state, and will wake feeling calm, settled, and at peace. Although the healer will have concentrated on the physical body, he/she will also, and again using in a constructive way the energy that has been created, have been aware of and given healing to the spirit self, the light of the soul.

In the same way, using mind energy connected with universal, God energy, we can give absent or distant healing. Projecting our thoughts forward and by concentrating our healing thoughts out toward a patient, those thoughts that are pure energy, healing energy, will travel through time and space to reach the person to whom it is directed. Healing, healing energy, knows no bounds. No distance is too far; our organization has many patients around the world who benefit from the healing we send to them.

There are so many stories that I could relate, some sad, many funny, all inspirational, and maybe one day I will write a book dedicated to healing alone, to the patients and to the healers, to my students who are all so wonderful in their giving, and, of course, to those in the spirit world who guide and help us in the work that we do. But one story I will tell here, a story that is ongoing and begins for us, the Rosemary Altea Association of Healers (RAAH), some seven years ago.

Liz Hornby had read in the local newspaper that our second healing center was to be opened in the town of Scunthorpe, in the north of England, close to her home.

Her son Mark, then aged twenty-two, had just twelve months previously been hit by a car as he was crossing the road. He had been knocked down and seriously injured, sustaining severe head injuries, and his parents had been informed by his surgeon that Mark would never be anything more than a vegetable for the rest of his life. For the first eight months after his accident he was in a coma; then, as he slowly came out of it, the doctors realized that his brain had not been totally damaged, that he could hear and understand, but was unable to respond in any way. The diagnosis was that this was the best that could be hoped for. This, under the circumstances, was a miracle in itself.

Finally the day came when Mark's parents took him home. There was no hope for a brighter future, but at least their son was alive. Liz Hornby's determination to help her son, even though the odds were stacked heavily against the kind of help she wanted, that great miracle that would heal her son, led her to the RAAH. She asked if we could help, and that first time I went along to assess Mark, and to decide which of our healers I should assign to this patient, is one that I will never forget. His spine injuries left this young man slumped in a wheelchair, unable to lift his head more than a fraction, unable to move his arms or his hands save one finger, spittle oozing from his mouth over which he had no control. As I talked to him he turned his head sideways in an effort to look at me, and I looked into his eyes, eyes that told me that he understood me . . . eyes that were smiling . . . eyes that were then laughing as I joked with him. And I knew then that Mark would be my patient. That somehow, no matter how busy my schedule, I would find the time to give healing to Mark.

I have mentioned that we in the RAAH work as a team, and it has been with the help of that team that we have been able to ensure that Mark has had a visit from one or more of us every week. One of our healers, Joan Mould, visits Mark with me regularly and takes on the responsibility of visiting him when I am out of the country.

Although he is still in a wheelchair, Mark is now talking and receiving speech therapy. He is doing remarkably well and is easily understood. He goes to college once or twice a week and is learning to use a computer, and he writes out all of his own Christmas and birthday cards.

About four years ago Mark was taken into the hospital for a thorough assessment. Although the surgeon was amazed at Mark's progress, Liz and Bob, Mark's parents, were told that it would be impossible for Mark to improve further, that he would never walk again, as part of his spine had crumbled as a result of his accident. The X-rays they had taken showed this clearly; therefore it would be impossible for Mark to stand and support his weight. However, God moves in mysterious ways. Mark is now learning to walk again and is doing very well. Not just a step or two, quite a bit more than that. His balance is a bit of a problem at the moment, and he needs some support, but as he grows stronger and builds his confidence, who knows what he may achieve? He has already beaten all the odds.

There have been many people, friends, carers, doctors, and the like, who have given help to Mark and his family, and Mark has been given encouragement by many, not least his mother, a brave and courageous woman who has quietly battled to attain a good quality of life for her son. Mark, too, has battled and is winning this battle.

My organization is just one small cog in a wheel that just keeps on turning. But that one small cog, with God's help, can from time to time produce miracles.

Before including their story in this book, I asked Mark and his parents if they would like to add anything to what I had written. Knowing that this book would be published and knowing that their story would be read by many people, some in the same situation as themselves, Bob and Elizabeth Hornby asked me to add this comment:

"Rosemary, you gave us hope when everyone else gave us despair."

It can take but one man, one voice, to rock the world.

Mark is still laughing, and to me, this is the greatest miracle of all.

The
Power
within
Us

Accepting my role as a healer was difficult at first, but understanding that God and the universe create that power, that healing energy, makes it easier for me to pursue that role.

Discovering that power, and the meaning of that power, took many years, and still I know there is more for me to learn.

I am fortunate. Grey Eagle took me by the hand and led me gently to the place where I am now.

It was 1983. I was actually here, in one of the most fascinating countries of the world, mythical and mystical, Egypt—a place I had longed for some time to visit.

I was in Egypt to do some research into the lives of the ancient Egyptians. I needed to discover, if I could, how they were able to tap into those unseen energies that some of us refer to as psychic power.

I had read of the goddess Isis and of her abilities as a healer, and her story had intrigued me more than those of the many others I had heard about the ancient gods and goddesses of Egypt. In visiting her country, I hoped to come closer to her and to her spiritual beliefs and perhaps achieve a greater understanding of my subject and of my work as a medium.

I spent three weeks exploring ancient temples, old ruins, burial grounds, and museums. But it was not until after visiting the Pyramids, and actually exploring inside the largest of the three at Giza, that I was to experience for the first time that well-known psychic phenomenon, astral travel.

Astral travel . . . the ability of the etheric body to leave, to vacate, the physical body and move, travel, through time and space, in exploration. To travel through space, to go where there are no physical barriers and where anything is possible.

My trip inside the Pyramid was disappointing, and I came away with the distinct feeling of being let clown. Goodness knows what I expected to find or, more to the point, what I expected to feel. There were no shadows or ghosts from past times, no unknown voices whispering their stories. I saw no lights, felt no energies, and as I stood in the center of the Pyramid there was, for me, no tremendous surge of power such as I had imagined there might be.

It was as I was climbing back down the steep narrow passages on my way out that I asked Grey Eagle what, if anything, he thought I had gained from this experience.

He gave me one word: power.

I didn't understand him and was more disgruntled than ever as I came back out into the sunshine. It had been an exhausting day, and I arrived back at the apartment tired and hungry, determined not to think too much about the day's events until I had had a good night's sleep.

I woke in the middle of the night to find myself standing between the two single beds. Although it was dark in the room, there was a glimmer of light shining through the crack in the bedroom curtains that enabled me to see quite well. Everything looked and felt quite ordinary, and I experienced no weird sensations of any kind. Only moments passed before the thought flitted across my mind: What am I doing here? and automatically I turned my head, looking over my shoulder to where my bed was.

I wasn't shocked or surprised, only mildly intrigued to find myself peering down at the still and seemingly sleeping form occupying the bed I had only just got out of—the form I instantly recognized as me!

Another thought skimmed through my mind. This must be what it's like to be dead. I chuckled at the idea but knew it was nearly right, and then my curiosity got the better of me. I'll explore, I thought—and no sooner the thought than the deed.

As with the Pyramids, I cannot tell you what I expected to happen, but this time I knew that something would.

I've heard many people talk about the speed of light, but to me it had always been a meaningless phrase . . . until now. I was aware that I was moving (to say "traveling" would be more accurate), and I was also aware of the tremendous speed, but it was all so natural and so easy. I wasn't flying or floating, and no effort at all was required, yet here I was traveling—astral traveling.

Within a short space of time, and time of a different concept from that I can put into words, I found myself in a large, brightly lit room, surrounded by people. Everyone was chattering, lively and seemingly enjoying what appeared to me to be some sort of party. I felt welcome and warm, not in the least nervous or afraid, but excited, very excited.

It wasn't a dream, as some of you may be thinking, nor was it an overactive imagination. I gazed around me and knew for sure that this was real.

I could fill a book by just recounting the events of that one night. But that, maybe, is for another time. All I can do here is give you just a small glimpse of the probabilities in another world, in another dimension, and in another time.

The people I met that night seemed to be real and of solid matter, flesh and bone, so to speak. They were of varying ages and dressed as one might expect to dress for an informal party.

Shaking hands with them was exactly the same as shaking hands with someone in our world. I felt myself to be solid also, with just the same physical form I had left behind.

Probably the one thing that impressed me the most about my visit into this other realm was the colors. Everything was so fresh, so clean and clear, making the colors stand out beautifully. I don't mean just the color of the sky or the grass or the flowers in the gardens. Even the colors of the women's dresses seemed to hold more clarity.

Many times I had read about other people's experiences into the astral planes, and I have been asked lots of times by clients or patients, "Do you believe it?"

Before that night, I was able to answer only that I thought it might be possible. Since my first experience I have been astral traveling many times, and I have always had that same clear vision and knowledge of what is happening to me.

One time, quite soon after this first experience, I woke one morning early. I was at home, in Yorkshire, England, and automatically I searched for the bedside clock hoping that it wasn't yet time to get up. It was 6:00 A.M. Oh, good, I thought. I've got a couple more hours. I snuggled down in the bed again. But then I felt that old familiar feeling that told me something was about to happen. This time, though, as my body began to shake and the feeling inside grew like a volcano about to erupt, I determined that I would put a stop to whatever or whoever it was that seemed to be taking me over. Gritting my teeth, my mind screaming out to Grey Eagle for help, and with great effort I managed to retain control of my body. Forcing myself into a sitting position and breathing a sigh of relief, I plumped up my pillows and lay back, now fully awake and alert. I looked again at the clock, which now said 6:15 A.M. precisely. Only seconds later, however, I was regretting that I had put a stop to what I now felt had been an opportunity to go traveling. I knew that Grey Eagle had been with me and still was, so a little hesitantly but determined for the experience, I said to him, "Okay, let's go. But just remember, I don't want to go too far away."

I relaxed my body, and before I knew it that feeling began again, like a motor starting up somewhere deep inside me, and I started to shake. This time, feeling safe with Grey Eagle beside me, I allowed the energy to grow. Then I was moving, so fast that I could feel the "flesh" pulled back from my face and my teeth bared as a force of great magnitude drove me forward. On and on I went, seemingly through a long dark tunnel, until finally I found myself standing just inside the entrance to a passage. For just a brief moment I had the sensation that I was a small child around the age of seven years, and I seemed to be blind in one eye; but that feeling dispelled quickly, and I was me again, full and able-bodied, appearing flesh and bone. It took a moment for my mind to comprehend the scene I faced. It seemed too incredible, and I was so excited and amazed that it was all so really real. I looked out upon a marketplace, with market stalls and cobbled stones and people, many, many people, milling about, shopping, chatting, laughing, shouting, just like any ordinary busy market day scene with lots of hustle and bustle. But there were some differences. All the people were dressed in Victorian-style clothes, and the buildings were obviously of the same era; in fact, it was just like stepping into a Dickens novel . . . with two exceptions. First, everything was clean and spotless. The women's dresses were not muddied and soiled as they should have been. The marketplace was free of litter or any kind of rubbish. Second, the colors were like none I had ever seen here on the earth plane, so bright, so clear, and defined.

I stepped out of the tunnel and began to walk slowly through the crowd, turning first to smile at one, then to say hello to another of the people there. None responded to my greetings (did I walk through their world as if a ghost?), but it mattered not to me, for I was so involved in the experience, so thrilled.

As I walked on, my eyes were drawn to a row of shops to my left, and my amazement grew to incredulity. My jaw must have dropped a foot at least as what I saw registered in my brain. A sign above a shop doorway, a sign that read "Rosemary Susan Edwards (Lacemaker)," stared back at me. I knew that I was here, I did not recognize the place, but I knew I was not dreaming. I knew that I had come here via astral travel, and I knew that there was something here to learn. Maybe I had lived here in another life, maybe another time. This was something I had to think about, but one thing I knew for sure was that the shop sign connected with me in some way, for my maiden name was Rosemary Susan Gail Edwards.

Without realizing it, as these thoughts were swimming around in my head I had continued to walk, through the crowd to the edge of the market square. Now I found myself approaching a small arched bridge. On either side of the opening to the bridge stood two ladies. They were dressed totally differently from the others I had seen, and I felt they did not belong somehow. They were very tall, quite large boned, with blond hair pulled back severely from their faces. They wore plain pale gray dresses tied with a cord around the middle.

With some enthusiasm, for my instincts told me that these two would acknowledge my presence, I went forward onto the bridge. The two women followed me, one on either side, and as I walked I asked them, "Tell me, please, can you tell me where I am?"

The lady on my right, in answer to my question, replied, "I'll give you a clue: you are on the A twenty-one." (In England we have "A" roads, "B" roads, and "M" roads.)

Without realizing it, I had placed my hands on the parapet of the bridge, and as she spoke, the lady placed her hand gently but firmly over my right hand. The shock of feeling *flesh on flesh*—for this was the first time throughout this experience that I had had any sensation of physical contact—threw me off balance. I stared down at her hand on mine and panicked.

"I want to go back," I called to Grey Eagle, and the next thing I knew I landed with a thud, back in my body, in my own bed, staring at the place I had come from.

Over in the corner of the room, close to the ceiling, I

could see what I knew to be the entrance to the tunnel I had just traveled through—a circular moving mass of energy, perfectly round. The only way I can think to describe this energy is for you to visualize a swarm of bees, varying degrees of gray in color, making the buzzing sound that a swarm of bees makes. This is what I saw and heard, and with absolute certainty I knew that somehow I had come from there. I looked at the clock: it registered 6:30 A.M. The whole experience had taken just fifteen minutes—fifteen minutes, that is, if we gauge time by our standards. But I have learned over the years that time in the spirit world is not measured in the same way that it is here on earth.

I cannot begin to express the excitement I felt about this experience, and I could hardly wait to tell my friends about it. As fantastic as it seems, it really happened, and I have been on many other astral journeys since that time.

Do I understand it? No, not entirely. Do you, the reader? I doubt it very much, but although we may be puzzled as to the way some things work, that doesn't mean they don't happen. Seeing is not always believing, but experiencing things firsthand is. I believe!

It would, of course, have been unthinkable to leave Egypt without visiting the Valley of the Kings and the Valley of the Queens, so I flew down from Cairo to Luxor for four days.

Never have I visited a more fascinating place, and I discovered there, through my research, just how important the ancient Egyptians considered the afterlife to be. So many of their beliefs tied in with my own that I felt a compatibility grow between us, stronger than time and space, born of a likeness of mind.

It was in Luxor that I began to understand what my guide Grey Eagle had meant by "power"—his answer when I had asked what he thought I had gained by visiting the Pyramid.

I had been staying at the palace of the old King Farouk, which, many years ago had been turned into a hotel. My bedroom was large and comfortable, and the view was magnificent. Tall French windows opened onto a small balcony overlooking the river Nile, and across the river, almost close enough to touch, were the great and mysterious-looking hills, behind which lay the burial grounds of the ancient kings and queens of Egypt I had come so far to see.

Often during my short stay in Luxor, I had stood on the balcony outside my bedroom window, looking down on the river below. It fascinated me to watch the boats, some large, some small, and most of them in need of repair. The "floating hotels," which took tourists on their trip of a lifetime, looked as if they would sink if one or more of their passengers sneezed too hard. But it was the little sailing boats, the feluccas, that really drew my attention. I decided that come what may, I would have a trip on one of those before I flew back to Cairo.

Now this sounded like quite a simple thing to organize, and listening to the young boys who sailed the feluccas, I should have done it on my first day. They wanted only the tourists' money, my money, but what they didn't tell you was that there was no wind, and no wind meant no sailing. For four days all the little sailing boats lay idle, by the river-banks. The young boys became more and more desperate, pestering any and every tourist they saw, making it impossible for visitors to take a quiet stroll along the river.

Then came my last day in Luxor, and wind or no wind, I felt I had to keep my promise to myself. The two boys I approached, both of them only in their early teens, couldn't believe their luck and hurried me aboard their small vessel before I changed my mind. For twenty very boring minutes one of the boys pushed the boat along with the aid of a long pole, while the younger of the two pulled us along by grabbing hold of the many boats moored by the side of the river.

"This won't do," I eventually grumbled to myself, and asked the boys if they would put up the sail and try it that way. After all, there was nothing at all exciting about being pulled and pushed along the Nile.

With exaggerated patience, the older of my two "sailors" explained in broken English the uselessness of a sail without wind, adding with polite assurance that if he could make the wind blow, of course he would, but alas, he could not.

"Well, that's it, then," I stated quite confidently, adding without a thought of what I was saying: "If you want the wind, then I will make the wind."

Immediately I became still and spoke to my guide, sending up a silent request to Grey Eagle, positively asking for a wind to blow through the sails on the little boat to make it dance across the water. Silent and still I sat, gazing ahead to where my guide was, and I concentrated all my energies toward helping him. Not once did I doubt that my request would be granted, and sure enough, about ten minutes later I began to see results.

At first I felt a gentle breeze, lightly touching my cheeks, and then fingers playing through my hair. Then the river began to sing as the wind, stronger now, skimmed through the water like stones. Suddenly a gust of wind caught at the sails of our little boat, which had been loosely furled, and they struggled to break free. Seconds later, for as far as the eye could see, the river came alive. With shouts and yells of glee, the natives brought their vessels into the water. Laughing, waving, they called to each other. The waiting was over, Allah was good to them, and they could work again.

The sails now up and blowing full and free in the wind, we went out into the middle of the river. It was glorious and exhilarating, and I chuckled as I watched the busy scene, everyone noisy and happy.

But my crew were silent, a look of doubt and uneasiness on their faces. The older of the two turned a searching, questioning gaze upon me, and I answered his silent inquiry. Looking directly into his eyes, smiling gently, I said quietly: "You wanted the wind, I gave it to you."

For the remainder of the excursion they were subdued, talking to each other only when necessary, every now and then sending furtive glances my way. And difficult though it was in the confined space we had, forced as they were to struggle for control of the sails, they made sure not to come within three feet of me, at least.

Much later, when I was alone in my room, I thought hard about what had happened and began seriously to contemplate the power and energy it takes to create this kind of phenomenon. In the Pyramid, Grey Eagle had told me that I had gained power, and I hadn't understood.

I think what he really meant was that I had gained knowledge of the power that I already had—the power that all of us possess, the power of the mind. It was up to me now, with his help, to harness that power and to use it in the best way possible—to do God's will. To help me in my daily life and to help me to help others.

Above all else, it must be remembered by all those who have learned to harness such power as this, myself included, that respect of this power is all important.

There is no doubt that through the ages there have been men and women with great power, their own power, people who have used and abused this to control others. It is more than possible to control or influence another's mind, especially if that mind is weak, and it is also possible not only to be constructive and creative, but to be destructive, too. History tells its own tales, of powerful and cruel men and women, kings and queens, holy men, tyrants and rulers, who have used their strength in negative and destructive ways. It also tells of powerful men and women who have been creative and good. All these people have one thing in common: they know their own power, they have known how to use it, they have understood the power of the mind . . . the most powerful and creative possession we all own.

The power I possess, combined with the power of the universe, enables me to be what I am, to dare to be, to dare to be myself. I have made a vow, a promise to God, to the universe, to all of those in the spirit world. I made this vow a long, long time ago, and it is this. Whatever you may call it, this power that I have, this gift to see, to hear, to communicate, to travel, to heal, I will use this power for good and in the way that the universe demands is the right way—in a way that will heal and ease hearts, bring joy and light and, I truly hope, enlightenment.

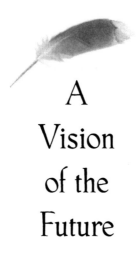

A
Vision
of the
Future

Having talked of astral travel, and of the power within us, I will now talk of how using that power enables me to see— and to see the future.

But how do I begin this chapter? Knowing that this aspect of my gift is such a curiosity to so many people, knowing that there is a need for some kind of explanation, how do I begin?

Many ancient cultures around the world, aware of the value of "dreams," encourage the telling of dreams to their seer, for his or her interpretation. A dream could be of great importance to a young man wishing to know if he should be a hunter, a warrior, or a craftsman. A dream to a young woman could tell of a future husband and happiness. Such was the importance of dreams that some American Indian tribes would send out their young men, when they reached a certain age, either into the sweat lodge or into the desert, to seek a dream, to seek a vision. Some would meditate, others might adopt a sleep or trance state, and it was not unusual, when seeking a vision, to use hallucinatory substances.

They would send their young men on a "vision quest" to seek their future. The interpretation of such dream visions was left to the wise man of the tribe, and that interpretation would determine the young man's future. Moreover, the wise man, seer, or shaman would also use this same exercise from time to time, for a successful vision quest would give him great clarity and aid him not only with his own learning and understanding, but also in giving help and advice to those members of his tribe for whom he was responsible.

My guide has spoken many times to me of this, and so it was that Grey Eagle, shaman, spiritual leader of his tribe, would use this power, the power to "see" that which the future held, not just for himself, but for others, too. Sometimes he would know, without knowing how. Often he would have a vision with no effort on his part to receive one, and on occasion, needing more clarity, he would embark upon a vision quest, and he would discover the "future."

Many books are written on shamanism, some good, some bad. Some will give instructions to the layperson on how to become a shaman. Read them if you will, believe them if you will, but let me make clear what I believe, what I have been taught, knowing that some will disagree. Only a true shaman can teach a shaman. Only a true shaman can guide another, teach another, to become a true shaman, and this training will take years, perhaps even a lifetime, before the student can claim to be a shaman also. There is much mystique and mystic power, and enlightenment in the ways of the shaman is a slow process.

And so it is that Grey Eagle, shaman, has taught his student—not with instant success, often with rigorous lessons, but always with immense patience and understanding for his student's shortcomings, which are many, and always acknowledging and gentle with his student's human frailties.

And so it is, that I the student, medium and healer, often impatient, lacking understanding, angry and less than gentle with myself for my human frailties, demanding and often expecting too much too soon; and so it is, with time and patience, that Grey Eagle, shaman, has taught his student.

It is easy for me to "see" another's future, for those in the spirit world will often give help and advice through me to those they love, advice regarding future prospects, new and forthcoming opportunities, choices. Sometimes they will show me the inevitable and inescapable path that a person will walk along. Grey Eagle is always there to show a clear pathway, if it is felt by those in the spirit world that this is necessary and that a person will benefit from this kind of guidance. At times, though, this door will be closed, and knowledge of the future will be withheld, inaccessible, for it may be considered by those in the spirit world that to divulge this information would be harmful or unnecessary to a person and may serve only to muddle or confuse. Or it may be considered that to tell too much would be detrimental to the learning process. There are certain answers that each must discover for himself, for it is in seeking out these answers that one grows. But more often than not I will talk to my clients of their future, not dictating a way of life, but rather allowing them to see their own potential, helping them to discover a door they had not yet realized was there, showing them an opportunity and giving them the confidence to make the most of it. Giving hope where there was none, confidence where there was a lack of it, warnings of care to be taken when haste may wreak havoc.

Born with the power to see, I have been taught by Grey Eagle to use my gift with great caution and with the utmost responsibility, for there are those who would allow me to dictate their every move, run their lives. And there are some who, knowing and having experienced the accuracy of this power I own, would (if I allowed them) pile the responsibilities of their lives upon me, instead of making their own decisions and being responsible for themselves.

Grey Eagle has taught me well, and as a medium I am very aware of the great effect I have upon each individual who seeks me out. I know that I can change a person's life . . . have indeed changed many people's lives. And so I treat my gift with caution and with great care, knowing that this gift is a God-given one.

From the most trivial to the more serious issues, I have learned that there is always a good reason why we are given information about the future, and if we use that information wisely, we can benefit greatly from it.

I remember once, as in a vision, I saw a friend's car, parked by the side of the road with a flat tire. Knowing that the next day she was going to see her mother and that the journey was a fairly long one, around two and a half hours, I decided to tell her what I had seen and advised her to get her tires checked before she went. Both her husband and her son were car mechanics, and they went over the car with a fine-tooth comb, finding no problems whatsoever. But she had been warned, and taking notice, she took a more than steady drive to her parents' home, instead of her usual fast pace. All went well, and they arrived safely at their destination. After the very necessary cup of English tea, she and her family decided to take a walk to stretch their legs. Out the door they went, past the car that was parked at the side of the road . . . with a totally flat tire.

Now, no one can really say that an accident had been prevented. No one can assume that had my friend driven at her usual speed, the tire might have burst, causing the car to leave the road. No one really knows. But my friend Joan, well, I can tell you . . . she is in no doubt at all.

Such a trivial issue, one that might or might not have become much less trivial if Joan had not listened.

Of course I help, with the aid of those in the spirit world, and give guidance with so many different aspects of life, some of which I have already discussed throughout this book, and although I accept the fact which is that many people are able to glimpse the future in one way or another, the accuracy, the preciseness of detail in many cases of the information which I am able to give, still astounds and amazes me and makes it impossible, thank goodness, for me to become complacent, which is no bad thing. I do not pretend to know how it works, and I freely admit that I do not have all the answers, far from it. I am not all knowing and all seeing for all my gift may suggest that this is so. For all that I *do* know, I know that there is *more* to know, more to learn, much, much more. I am aware that being merely mortal gives me limited concepts, and so I try not to presume that A times B equals C; to do so would be to place limitations on the power of the universe, which has no limitations.

Again, with regard to messages of future events for others, I was once a guest in the late 1980s on a BBC radio show. It was at the time of the International Around the World Yacht Race, and the presenter of the show, while talking to me in the studio, was also talking by radio phone to some of the members of the British Yacht Team. Naturally he asked me if I had any advice to give them. My answer was instant, for even as I was being asked this question Grey Eagle was talking to me.

"I know nothing of yachts and sailing," I said, aware that the show was live and that there would be thousands of listeners, "but I am told to advise you that there will be some problem with the engines or engineers, and I am also being told to tell you to be careful near the side of the boat." And I repeated, "I can clearly see a problem with either engines or engineers and the side of the boat."

Well, as I relayed this message and my voice crackled down the radio receiver to the members of the yacht team, I could hear their laughter as they explained to me, with good humor, that yachts don't have engines. They were obviously not taking me one little bit seriously, which was a great pity. Had they listened, had they taken notice, maybe, just maybe, a tragic accident might have been avoided.

Just a few days later, out at sea, one of the engineers fell over the side of the yacht and was drowned.

One year later I was invited back to the same BBC radio show with the same interviewer, Charlie Partridge, who was now much more responsive and enthusiastic about the work I do and listened with new eagerness.

For the thousands of clients I have, there are thousands of stories I could relate where information from the spirit world regarding future events has given comfort, hope, and inspiration to so many. One in particular sticks in my mind, a tale that has its own telling ending . . . and a hopeful and beautiful message for us all.

I had not seen this lady before, and I cannot even remember her name, so for the purposes of this story, I will call her Eva. This was not the first time Eva had sought out someone to tell her her future, but she had never before been to a medium. So she was first shocked and then delighted to find herself suddenly communicating with her parents, who had died some several years earlier.

Eva was in her early sixties, well and healthy in body but emotionally in great distress, as her parents were quick to explain to me. One day Eva came home from work to find her husband gone. He had taken all his belongings and, leaving a brief note, had disappeared. Eva was naturally devastated and confused, as she had thought her marriage of over thirty-five years a happy one. In the intervening three years she had heard not one word from her husband. All she could see for herself in her future was a life of misery and loneliness, for she knew she would never again trust any man enough even to consider starting up a relationship, let alone get married.

I was immediately sympathetic toward Eva and asked Grey Eagle if he could help this lady, perhaps give her some hope for a better future.

As in a vision I saw, much to my delight, that as unbelievable as it might seem to Eva, her life, her future, was going to be a happy one.

I was shown a path, Eva's path, which at first was dark and narrow. I saw Eva walking along this path with her head down, her shoulders drooped, miserable and without hope. She walked along this path, with heavy steps and heavy heart, but then I watched her approach a turn in the road— and suddenly, so suddenly, it was as if the sun had come out. The light was very bright and told of a future that was fulfilled and incredibly beautiful. As I recounted what I had seen to Eva, I was so enthusiastic in my description that a ray of hope came into her eyes. She cried and asked if I really thought this was possible. I was in no doubt, for what I had seen was so clear, and I told her so.

"October," I said, "only ten months away. I know that ten months seems a long time to wait, but it will go quickly, and then . . . well, then, my dear, the sun will come up, your life will change completely, and you will find the most unbelievable happiness." Eva was thrilled and hopeful, and as her son drove her home, she recounted all that she had been told.

The following November, eleven months later, Eva's son rang to thank me for giving his mother such a wonderful message, a message filled with joy. It had enabled her to live a happier life, since she had come to believe that her life would change for the better—which it had, her son then said.

"Finally," he told me, "she is happy and at peace, for we buried her a month ago."

Eva had suffered a sudden heart attack in October and had died instantly. Her path had indeed taken a turn, and as she had walked along that path the sun had at last begun to shine.

I will often know whether my patients with serious illnesses will recover or if they will pass over into the spirit world. This is a hard part of my work as a medium and healer, for I get to know my patients well, and because I hold the answers to many questions relating to life after death, there are those patients who are terminally ill who I develop a close relationship with.

One such patient was Margery, who had suffered with cancer for some time before arriving at one of my centers with her husband one evening. As I spoke with Margery that night, I knew, I could "see," that she was going to die, that no matter what she or I or anyone else did, she would soon go through that door marked death, to continue her journey on in another world.

Over the months that followed I became very close with my patient, and I knew that she was so afraid to die. But, brave and battling, she rarely let this fear show through. Even when she had less than two weeks to go and knew the battle was nearly over, she still, with dignity, showed herself to be brave. I visited her every day, and after giving her healing, I would sit for an hour or two, sometimes talking, sometimes quietly holding her hand. Then one time, just a few days before she left us, as I walked up to the house the door opened. The doctor was just leaving, and Tony, Margery's husband, said, "Just go straight up, Rosemary, I'll be a little while with the doctor. "

Now Margery had heard the doctor leave, but she did not know that I had arrived. Thinking that she was on her own, she began to cry, to beg, to plead, "Dear God, dear God, I don't want to die." I heard her scream, "Please, please, God, don't let me die!"

I had already begun to climb the stairs, and as I reached the top I could see into the bedroom. I could see Margery, leaning half out of her bed, clutching hold of the bedside chair, hysterical, terrified, and begging for help, I knew that the last thing she would want was for me to see her in this state, so I turned to go back down the stairs. Just then she looked up and saw me standing there. Straight away she stopped her crying, knowing that I had heard her but wanting desperately to cling to her dignity. For the one thing that Margery had always told me was that she was afraid that she might die with no dignity at all. Her hair was gone, but she wore a wig day and night, refusing to take it off; her face was yellow and bloated; but still she was a proud and dignified woman.

I went toward her, holding out my hands, and she took them, over and over saying how sorry she was, that she hoped she had not upset me, concerned now only for me and for my feelings. We talked for a long while, and it was to be the last time that Margery was able to talk to me in this way, for soon after she slipped into a coma. She told me then of another fear. She was scared, she explained, that when she finally escaped her physical body she would get lost, not be able to find her way toward the light.

"How would you feel if I came with you?" I heard myself say. "I can't promise, but I could try. Would that make you feel easier?"

"But can you do that?" she replied, her voice full of hope and relief.

I looked to Grey Eagle, who answered my silent question to him. "Yes," I said, "I'm pretty sure I can, and if it will help you, then I'll gladly come along with you."

Now this was a pretty unusual thing for me to suggest. I had been astral traveling many times and for a variety of reasons. Also, in my rescue work, helping distressed souls to cross the void that separates worlds, I had often experienced exciting journeys to many places and met many wonderful people. And, too, there had been those times when a patient of mine had "died" and I had, in one way or another, been there with them. But this was the first time I had actually spoken with a patient about the possibility of joining her on her final journey into the spirit world.

Astral travel is something many people experience. Although amazing, it is not unusual, and this was how I intended to join Margery on her journey. Grey Eagle was behind me one hundred percent, knowing that this was what was needed.

When I left Margery's house that day, she was much brighter, less afraid, feeling that she really was not on her own. A few days later we went together on a journey.

In the early hours of that particular morning, with my physical body still in my bed, I found myself in a very large room, as large as a good-size ballroom, with two rows of chairs, back to back, placed down the middle. I was seated at one end right at the bottom, and all the other chairs were filled. Lots of people, lots of chatter, lots of noise, as everyone seemed to be waiting excitedly for something to happen.

As I sat, curious about my surroundings, I became aware that I had caused some considerable interest in a few of the people at the other end of the room, who were whispering to each other and pointing to where I sat. One or two of their faces were familiar to me, but I could not bring to mind where it was that I had seen them before.

While I was pondering this thought, there was a sudden, expectant hush and then a whispering of excited voices: "She's here, she's coming, she's coming!" I looked to one side of the room, where everyone else was looking, and noticed for the first time a kind of chute sticking out of the wall. Then, before I had time to wonder what this was, I saw a woman appear through the hole in the wall, along the chute, to land gently with her feet safely on the ground.

I knew her, but for a moment I could not place her, and I watched as the people who had been waiting at the top end of the room went forward with open arms to greet her. Then recognition dawned. It was Margery . . . but not the Margery I had known. This Margery did not wear a wig, and her hair, healthy and shining, fell about her shoulders. Her face, not yellow and bloated, was full of vitality, and she was vibrant. The difference in her was amazing. I also realized that the people who had been pointing toward me were the very ones I had talked to many times when Margery had been on the earth plane. They were her parents and her family in the spirit world, who I had communicated with so often.

Sometime later I found myself back in my body, and less than thirty minutes after that the phone rang. It was around six-thirty in the morning, and it was Margery's husband, Tony, calling to tell me that Margery had died less than an hour ago.

I was able to tell Tony of my experience, and this comforted him greatly. It also helped me to know that when I do foresee death, what I truly see is new life beginning.

Seeing into the future for others is one thing, seeing for myself is another. I have from time to time, with Grey Eagle, embarked upon a vision quest or have been given a dream vision by Grey Eagle, which will help me greatly to clarify my position, give me guidance as to the path that I am on and on which I must walk. And although these visions are very personal to me, I will recount to you just one, which I experienced in April 1993. In doing so, however, I must point out that a dream vision will sometimes be given in a symbolic way, as you will see.

I was on a boat, a strange-looking craft, long and tapering to a sharp point at the front end, with a small cabin in which I was seated, along with several others. A good friend of mine, Lynn Picard, an American I had met while working in Hong Kong, was with me, and as we were talking I suddenly noticed, through a porthole on the far side of the cabin, what looked to be a large mountainous hunk of red rock (it reminded me of the great red rocks you see in Arizona), rising out of the water. I got up and went across the cabin to the porthole to have a closer look and was totally awestruck at the sight that met my eyes. I went forward onto the deck, hardly able to grasp the most magnificent sight, for I saw icebergs, masses and masses of gigantic mountains of ice, some of them red, some gray, some white, a great multitude of floating ice for as far out from where we had come as the eye could see. It was a sight of such magnitude that my mind struggled with the fact that we had somehow come through this beautiful but so dangerous sea unharmed.

I turned toward the front of the boat and gasped as I saw that we were not yet out of danger, for there were icebergs to either side of us. I held my breath as the boat maneuvered its way through the narrow passageway, barely missing the icebergs, which, as we traveled on, seemed to grow smaller and smaller.

As the ocean became clearer, although the icebergs, behind us now, were still clearly visible, I became aware of yet another danger: as we approached the shore I saw bodies, hundreds and hundreds of bodies, floating facedown in the water. At first I thought they were dead bodies, but as we came closer I saw that these bodies were floundering, trying to stay afloat . . . but the boat I was on was heading straight toward them, making for the shore. At one point, as the boat speeded up, I thought we were going to hit the body of a young boy (don't ask how I knew that it was a boy, I just knew), but at the last minute a large wave lifted him up and carried him to the side of the boat.

Then, before I knew it, we came out of the water and

safely onto the beach. A little uncertain, I stepped off the boat and onto the shore, surprised to find, not sand beneath my feet, but solid ground. I stood for a moment or two, gazing out at the ocean, marveling at the miracle of navigation that had seen us safely, and without harm to others, through the torrent of icebergs and bodies that I could clearly see. I shook my head, incredulous at the sight of the sea I had left behind. Someone, a man, came and stood to the side of me. "Let me get you a drink," he said. Taking firm hold of my arm, he steered me toward a bar, and pouring a "special" glass of wine, he said, "This calls for a toast. . . . You've made it, you're safe."

When I came to, I knew immediately the meaning of the dream.

The icebergs were symbolic of the traumas and difficulties that had been my life's journey thus far. The bodies, floundering and all at sea, were symbolic of the many people I have yet to meet upon my journey into my future, people who will look to me for help, people who may feel that they are drowning and lost.

The boat indicating my journey, and the sea, telling of other lands.

The shore, not sand but firm ground, telling me not only of a safe arrival, but of a new land, new beginnings, and solid territory.

The man, not one special man, perhaps, but again symbolic of the acceptance of mankind for who I am and what I do.

And I knew also, when "waking" from this vision quest, that something important was about to happen, to change my life forever. Soon, very soon now, in another land, another shore, my work would truly begin.

It was in November, just seven months later, that I was introduced to an American literary agency. Shortly after I signed a contract with them, this manuscript was bought by publishers around the world.

My dream vision told it all!

PART V

The

Message

Our
Learning

"Grey Eagle teaches me."

I have used this phrase so many times throughout this book, and you must want to ask the question, "How?"

Knowing I will not be able to ease your curiosity (for my answers will only serve to make you more curious), I will attempt to give at least some small explanation.

I wake in the morning, open my eyes, and see him. He stands waiting, waiting for the day to begin.

My first question must be, What did I dream?

I can't remember, and so I look to Grey Eagle for the answer. I know he will not give it, but I ask him just the same.

Patiently he looks at me. The ball, I know, is back in my court.

And so the day goes, a million questions in my head, but

only a handful asked. The results the same, as my guide waits patiently and hands the questions back to me.

Slowly, with much frustration, I learn. The answers to my questions lie within. There is nothing I can ask that I do not, somewhere within the deep recesses of my soul, know the answer to.

This is the beginning of my apprenticeship.

Months pass by.

I talk more and more with those in the spirit world as my clientele grows.

At first using signs, symbols, most of which I instantly know the meaning of, not knowing how I know. Without realizing it the speed of my communication with the spirit world increases, my vision, my hearing, my senses, become sharper. The need for symbols lessens, but I am unaware of the change. It is only on reflection that I see this.

We sit, Grey Eagle and I, and he tells me things. I learn by his example. I learn to be still, to listen to that small quiet voice within me. And as my senses become heightened, I become more sensitive to that energy that permeates time and space, that which we, in simple terms, call "psychic energy." I become finely tuned, a transmitter, sending out and receiving . . . sending out and receiving . . . sending out and receiving. . . .

This is my everyday reality. And I live my reality every day.

Years pass.

I am still a student, still learning. I discover that each moment of time is precious. Nothing, not one thought nor yet one deed is wasted. A casual conversation, never casual. A chance meeting, unavoidable. Coincidence, always planned. And in discovering these things, I discover a great plan. A universal plan. I find, with great delight, that I am part of that plan. That all life form, and even that which seems to have no life, is inescapably part of the plan.

We sit, Grey Eagle and I, and he tells me things. He takes me on many journeys. We travel by many routes and different means. I learn by his example.

I am a willing student, thirsting for knowledge but more patient now. And so I grow.

"And I behold the universe, and all it is, and all it ever has been, and all its power, is yours."

I hear Grey Eagle tell me this. Then I reply:

"And I behold the universe, and all it is, and all it ever has been, and all its power is ours. And yet belongs to no one."

I look to my guide, so strong, so powerful and wise.

His gentle nature calms and soothes me. I strive to be like him.

There is no magic potion that I or you can take that gives us wisdom. Only our experiences will teach us and then, only if we are truly willing to learn. We can read a million books whose words inspire us, will help to point us in a certain direction. But only the experience can give us true meaning to the written word.

So many times I am asked, "What is the purpose of our lives here on earth?"

And if I am to be your teacher, I must answer, "To learn—to grow."

And when, in frustration, I hear you ask, "How—and how?"

Then I must answer, "Look within."

•   •   •

What is the purpose of my work as a medium, what can I achieve?

The main purpose is to help those in the spirit world, to be their voice. In doing this, I know that so many of my clients, so many of those here on earth who have heard me speak, will have been transformed, allowed themselves to open up, have been awakened and have discovered light and enlightenment of the spirit.

Having made contact with the spirit world, each person has made a discovery and is inevitably transformed by it.

The voice of the spirit world is unanimous in talking of life as a learning experience, and that means not only life here on the earth plane, but life continuing after death.

Grey Eagle has taught me, and I have tried to teach others.

Each of us is born with the light within us, the light that is the light of the soul. If we choose to recognize and to nurture this light, then, when we die, we will go to the light, to be embraced by it.

If we choose to live in darkness, while on earth or after "death," if we choose to allow the light to diminish, then we choose a dark place. But always it is our choice.

I am saying that there are no fires of hell unless we choose it to be so.

There are those who would then argue, What is the point of being good if we can all embrace the light? And I would say, If we chose the light, we chose to take responsibility for those bad deeds we did on earth.

We are here first and foremost for the good of, for the growth of, the soul.

This world of ours, this material world, which we experience for such a short span of "time," has become a world where anger and frustration know no limits, where violence and aggression rule. A world where DOG EATS DOG.

And the eyes of the spirit world are sad.

I look to Grey Eagle and ask, What can we do?

Does it have to be like this?

He answers, No. But it is your choice. Yours . . . and yours . . . and yours.

He answers, No. But each man, each woman, each child, must do his or her part. It is for you to choose, and you . . . and you . . . and you.

And the eyes of the spirit world are sad.

I hear their collective voice. . . . They ask, Will you listen? Will you learn? Where is the willing student?

I look to Grey Eagle and ask, What is the key?

And with much feeling he replies, GENTLENESS. Your world needs GENTLENESS.

There is a new world waiting to be born—your world— awaiting a rebirth.

Each individual, man, woman, child, is the mother of the world, will cradle the world and will dictate its destiny.

And how, I ask my guide, do we nurture this child yet to be born?

He answers, With gentleness, and only with gentleness.

So many of us in this DOG EAT DOG world see gentleness and perceive weakness. We use phrases like "If you want to get on in life, get tough." Be ruthless . . . and yet to have "*ruth*" means to have pity or compassion. To be without *ruth*, to be *ruthless*, is damaging to the soul, damaging to the world. We see someone as tough, and we perceive strength, and we perceive power.

And so we live in this DOG EAT DOG world, condoning violence, all the while using harsh words and tough actions, teaching our children the art of ruthlessness.

And I ask Grey Eagle, How can we learn?

He answers, With gentleness, only with gentleness.

The definition of "gentleness" according to the *Concise Oxford Dictionary* is: "not rough, mild, or kind—especially in temperament, moderate, not severe or drastic, honourable, quiet, requiring patience, generous, courteous."

But we are mere mortals, and with our human faults and frailties, how can we hope to achieve the art of gentleness in the fullest sense of the word?

And as I write I hear Grey Eagle speak:

"Try, you can but try, and the universe shakes and becomes brighter—and we have hope."

I look to my guide, so strong, so powerful and wise.

His gentle nature calms and soothes me. I strive to be like him.

I see his gentleness, and I do not see him weak, I perceive great strength.

I see gentleness and I perceive power.

I learn by his example and dare to be gentle, too. First with myself, then with others.

It is so hard, for I too have been raised in this DOG EAT DOG world, and I am afraid. What happens when I fail, as I so often do? Then I remember: DOG EAT DOG . . . SOUL EAT SOUL.

There is a new world waiting to be born, each individual the mother of this world.

And, as I try, the universe shakes and becomes brighter— and *I* have hope.

And so the day goes, a million questions in my head, but only a handful asked.

I will share with you in this book just five questions, questions that many have asked. I will ask and give you Grey Eagle's answers. But don't be surprised if the answers he gives create more and more questions looking for answers.

Question: Grey Eagle, why is it that we mortals can be so cruel to each other sometimes?

Answer: I will laugh at the naiveté of this question, for of course you know the answer. And each child comes to the earth . . . must stretch, must open wide, must experience, must try many things . . . will test himself as well as others.

And what better testing ground than the playground in which your children will run and shout and laugh and cry?

And what better testing ground than that of the playground?

And each parent must educate his child and talk of sensitivity and tolerance.

Must talk of understanding and communication.

But there are many who do not do these things.

And so the child who will naturally test and stretch himself and others will look to his parents, will look to his teachers, will look to the adult . . . will not learn by your fine words, but will learn by example only.

And the parent who talks of tolerance, and yet shows none, will develop an intolerant child.

•   •   •

And the parent who talks of charity, but gives none, will develop a charityless child.

And the parent who talks of communication, but talks so much he fails to listen, will have a child who screams and shouts and yells and will not communicate.

And those small children are not cruel, but yet experiencing, developing, and growing.

And the cruel act and the cruel deed will come only by example.

For each child is beautiful, born pure.

And each child is born with GENTLENESS and sensitivity.

And each parent will have the opportunity to develop that sensitivity and that GENTLENESS.

But your fine words and your fine explanations will not be an influence upon the child, for the child's eyes will see all.

For children are knowing creatures.

And will learn by example only.

Question: Grey Eagle, if we pray for God's forgiveness, will He give it to us?

Answer: God will heed your request. He will look into your heart, and if this request is born of truth, and of love, and comes from the heart, then God will take you to Him.

•   •   •

But this truly is not a matter for God. For we will know, because we are wiser than you, that the important question here is, "Will you forgive yourself?"

For unless you can forgive yourself with humility, with kindness, with GENTLENESS, and with understanding for your own limitations . . . unless you can look into your heart and truly forgive yourself, then no matter who else says to you, "I absolve you of your sins," you will not be at peace.

For true peace comes from within.

Question: Grey Eagle, in a material world is it wrong to desire material things?

Answer: I will not talk to you here of right or wrong.

The use of these words does not apply.

I will only tell you that if you put material comfort above all things, then you will damage your growth.

And it is for you to choose whether you wish to do this or not to do this.

But nowhere is it written that a man cannot lie down and place his head on a comfortable pillow.

And nowhere is it written that a man may not place a fur wrap around him to keep himself warm.

Remember only, know only, that material wealth is no more a key to heaven than poverty.

• • •

Know only that when it is your time to leave the earth plane, and to begin your life anew, the wealth that you bring with you will be the wealth of learning that you have gained which is within your heart.

If a man may choose to have a silk cushion or a hard rock to lie his head upon, then why should he not choose the silk cushion?

And God will not judge him harshly.

And if a man may choose to swim in a blue lagoon, or to walk in a hot dusty desert, then would he not be foolish if he did not choose to swim in the blue lagoon?

There is no need for man to punish himself, to deprive himself of his comforts, except only if this deprives another and hurts another. And so, if your material comfort is important to you, then why should it not be so?

But remember this. And I will say this to you, and from my heart.

The most beautiful thing is the love of the heart.

The most beautiful thing is the ease of the heart and the comfort of the heart.

And if you deprive yourself of this one small thing, then do not be surprised if your silk cushion becomes tearstained.

And do not be surprised if the blue lagoon becomes muddied with the unseen blood which you have shed.

First, give to the heart, and all else will follow in its own time.

Question: Grey Eagle, how can we deal with our own hurt feelings while striving to understand another who seems to have wronged us?

Answer: In your world there are many who will refuse to accept responsibility for their own actions . . . and, first, you must be prepared to accept that responsibility.

Blame . . . fault . . . these are words that you will use.
A finger pointed at another in accusation.
A finger, often harshly, pointed at your own self in accusation.

Where is your GENTLENESS?

Where is the softness that the soul demands?

Where is the love . . . true loving, which comes from deep within?
A love of life . . . the love of your own soul?

Where is the stillness within you?
Do you believe that it is truly gone?
Do you question that it was ever there?

Oh, be still, my children . . . oh, be still . . . be quiet . . . and listen.
Your own soul, and the heartbeat of your soul, whisper

to you. . . . Be still, and do not fear this GENTLENESS . . . for without it, you will always blame . . . you will always judge.

Discover this GENTLENESS, which is your own true heart.

Look to yourself, in any given circumstance, before you should look to another.

Accept the responsibility of your soul and your own spiritual growth, for you and no other . . . have the power to be still.

Question: Grey Eagle, how best can we deal with life's crises?

Answer: So many of you here on the earth plane walk through your lives in darkness. You turn to the light briefly, in times of need, then turn away.

When you turn from the light, you turn away from God . . . and, inevitably, you turn inward, and you become closed . . . and you hold your pain to you . . . and then the seed of the soul cannot grow, for it needs light to grow.

Turn your face to the light, for in that light you will find warmth . . . you will find healing . . . and you will find love.

Accept that all things given are a gift to you and part of your learning process.

Take your courage in your hands and step into the light.

• • •

Turn your face to the sun and allow God's light to shine down upon you.

For you are children of God, and as children, if you reach out your hand, God will take it, and He will hold it firm, and He will steer you to a greater understanding of your own self . . . and He will give you His strength.

He will not stem the flow of tears, nor will He wash away your pain . . . but He will take you to His breast and comfort you.

Come, sit by my fire.

Hold out your hands to the flame and be comforted by the warmth of it.

But understand that there are many who keep this fire going.

My fire needs kindling.

My fire needs those of you who will labor . . . who will go out and collect kindling to place on the fire.

The fire is there for all, and there are many who will come and sit by the fire. They will warm themselves . . . they will feel comforted . . . and then they will turn away to continue their lives.

There are those of you who will come and sit by my fire, and you will marvel at the height of the flames and be grateful for the warmth that the fire gives out.

And when you are truly comforted, you will turn away and continue with your lives.

•   •   •

And then there are those of you who will come and sit by my fire, and you will see how tall the flames grow . . . and you gain comfort from the warmth of the flames. And when you have been comforted enough, there are those of you who will then recognize that if the fire is to continue burning, in order that the many should be comforted, then there is work to be done and kindling to be found.

Come, all of you, and sit by my fire.

We demand nothing from you.

We ask that you give nothing . . . except only if you want to do so.

Come, sit by my fire and listen to the wise words.
Listen to the crackle of the sticks as the heat of the flame burns through them.
Watch the sparks fly . . . each spark is a light . . . each spark is truth . . . each spark is a knowing.

Come, sit by my fire, and I will warm you. . . .

I look to my guide, Grey Eagle, and with gratitude in my heart that he should share his wisdom with me, I say to him:
"I am but a student . . . a willing student."

David

When answering the question "Why are we mortals so cruel to each other sometimes?" Grey Eagle says:

"And each of us must talk of *sensitivity* and *tolerance*, must talk of *understanding* and *communication*."

These last chapters show not only how cruel we mortals can be, but how cruel life itself can be. Yet what seems cruel can teach us of our sensitivity. What appears harsh can show us how easily we lack tolerance. What seems unfair can lead us to a greater understanding, and what confuses and muddles us will show the need for communication.

When David lived here on the earth plane, he was unable to communicate, but his experience of life here, his mortal life, taught him many things. This young man, I was to discover, was born brain-damaged and lived most of his life on this side bound to a wheelchair. Unable to walk or talk, or do anything for himself, David was totally dependent on his parents and his sister.

As he grew older it became more and more difficult for his parents, Mr. and Mrs. Harrison, to manage, but they refused to put their son into a home. It was important to them that they take care of David themselves, no matter how hard it was.

There are many people in the Harrisons' position who find themselves with a terrible decision to make. Do they struggle to keep their child at home, or do they put their child into care? Some parents find it impossible to cope with the problems that their disabled offspring bring and are forced through circumstance to send their children away. Others, like June Harrison and her husband, keep their children at home.

Neither way is easy, and the decisions can be heartbreaking. But for the Harrisons, keeping their son at home with them was a decision they never regretted.

As I talked to David at my first meeting with his mother, I realized, probably for the first time, that a child born mentally and physically handicapped is not incapable of seeing the world and the people in it in an ordinary way. The child's body and brain might be damaged, but the mind, as David showed me, remains intact.

My first close encounter with the handicapped was years ago, when I was fifteen, and, strangely, at the local mental hospital in Leicester where my grandmother had been a patient— The Towers.

The drama group to which I belonged at school was asked to entertain some of the more able patients. We were to give a performance of *Hiawatha*, and I had the lead part. I did not know then, nor did I discover until about two years ago, in 1992, that the *Song of Hiawatha* speaks of "Grey Eagle."

> Mystic songs like these, they chanted,
> "I myself, myself, behold me."

It is the great Grey Eagle talking
All the unseen spirits help me.

Of course, as you might expect, all the group made silly comments about visiting the "loony bin," and we all had a bit of a giggle about the whole thing. We must have seemed an insensitive bunch of silly schoolgirls.

It was only as the coach taking us approached the gates to the hospital grounds that my nerve began to crack a little. And my mother's words, spoken often in my childhood, came flooding into my head to haunt me once again:

"You'll end up like your grandma, in The Towers."

I gazed out of the window and up the long driveway toward the large, cold, and imposing-looking building ahead, and I shivered.

But as the coach pulled up to the front door and all the girls and the two drama teachers jumped up, such was the hustle and bustle of preparing for the show that I was drawn along with the rest of the crowd, with no time to think.

The play went well, very well, in fact. The audience applauded, and we were then invited to stay for tea. Having had the usual lecture that always preceded any school outing, about being representatives of the school and so on, we were all, naturally, on our best behavior.

We were shown into a large hall with trestle tables partway down one side on which there were sandwiches, cakes, and biscuits. All around the rest of the room were people, patients, our audience, seated on hard-backed wooden chairs.

As we stood, my little group of friends and I, in a huddle by the door, wondering what to do, a nurse came up to us and explained cheerfully that we were expected to chat with and try to make friends with our audience.

This was more difficult at first than it might seem, as some of the patients were quite withdrawn. One or two even burst into tears (I now know that these people must have been suffering from depression). But we soon got into the swing of things, and chatting to these strangers became easier.

Then I noticed a lone figure sitting all by herself right in the middle of the room. This lady was possibly in her mid- to late forties, although it was difficult to tell her exact age. She had obviously placed her chair as far as possible from everyone else, and she sat still and silent and strange, very definitely strange.

My friends by this time had also noticed her, but such was the feeling of oddness that emanated from her that not one of us wanted to approach her.

"Well, one of us ought to go," I remember saying, "so I'll do it."

As I walked toward this still and silent figure, the thing that struck me most was a feeling of the most incredible loneliness, not just for her, but for me as well. And as I drew closer her pain and despair seemed to creep over me, covering me like a blanket of fog.

Her hair was black, jet black with streaks of gray, and cut straight round as if someone had used a pudding basin. Dark, despairing eyes stared out of a face devoid of any emotion and bored straight through me. The dress she wore was navy blue with tiny white flowers, and in her hand she held a lighted cigarette.

So still did she sit that although the cigarette had burned down almost to her fingers, none of the ash had dropped off at all. The length of ash was as long as the cigarette had originally been. I stared at it in amazement. I had never seen anything like it before.

Deeply moved by this lonely creature, but also terrified, I

coughed nervously and tried to say hello. At first I could hardly speak, but, determined, I forced myself to make the required effort. For what seemed like an eternity I struggled to make some sort of conversation, but it was as if I were addressing a stone wall.

Nothing flickered, not an eyelash or a muscle. Not even the cigarette ash.

Then I felt a gentle touch on my shoulder, and a nurse said quietly, "It's no good, dear, she's not at home today."

As I walked back up the room to my school friends, I could feel the prickling at the backs of my eyes, the awful lump in my throat, and, worse still, the weight of hopelessness and helplessness upon my shoulders.

I don't remember the rest of my time in that hospital, but I do know that I was glad to get out of there. But the memory of that pathetic little lady will stay with me always.

The fear I felt with this lady is the same kind of fear I also felt when I was asked to visit the daughter of a client of mine. This child had had massive brain damage at birth and was in a special care unit at St. Catherine's Hospital in Doncaster in the north of England. Her mother warned me before I went that several kids in this unit, housing some of the worst handicap cases, were not a pretty sight.

When Samantha found out where I was going, she wanted to come along, and I tried to persuade her that it was not a good idea. I didn't know what we were likely to come up against, and being a protective mother, I didn't want my daughter to see the "ugly" side of life.

How wrong could I be!

Samantha, eleven years old at the time, was fine. It was I who had the problem coping.

Superficially, I did the rounds, saying all the right things, nodding and smiling in all the right places. But inside me was turmoil, panic; all I wanted to do was run, just run away from these deformed creatures. They weren't children, were they? It was even questionable whether some of them were human. Their bodies were so distorted.

Then, as I sat in the day room, waiting for my friend to finish her visit and wishing myself a thousand miles away, one of these creatures shuffled up to me on his bottom. He couldn't use his legs because they were so badly mangled. His arms and hands were twisted, as was his face, and to complete this picture of ugliness, his hair, thick and unruly, stuck out from his head in bright ginger spikes.

I pretended not to notice him, but to my horror his twisted fingers caught hold of my skirt and tugged. At the same time, out of his mouth came a moaning sound.

My heart began to thud loudly, banging in my chest. What was I to do? I tried to ignore him, but he was persistent and just kept on tugging. Then a nurse, passing by, said casually: "It's all right, love, he just wants you to button up his pajama jacket."

I froze. Oh no, not me. I couldn't, didn't want to—touch him.

But why?

A few moments later the same nurse came by again. "If you do his jacket up, love, he'll stop pestering you," she said.

Well, now I had no option but to cooperate. Tentatively I looked down on this ugly little creature and, gritting my teeth, reached forward and did up his buttons.

There now. That wasn't so bad, was it? I thought as I leaned back on my chair. The thumping in my chest had subsided, and the panic I had felt had eased—but then, oh no! The tugging began again.

I sat forward, looking straight at him this time, thinking that perhaps I ought to move, as it seemed the only way to get rid of him.

It was as I was about to put my thoughts into action that the boy gave another hard tug at my skirt; then, making a noise something akin to a loud chuckle, he hooked his thumb into one of the spaces between the buttons on his jacket and yanked hard. The jacket flew open, and a wicked grin spread across his twisted face as he tugged once more at the hem of my skirt. And I fell in love.

For the first time since I had been in that awful hospital, I laughed. It had become blatantly obvious that this funny little thing had been playing games with me. Wanting my attention, needing recognition. And because of his persistence, he had won.

The instant I laughed, his crooked fingers gripped his jacket and flapped it up and down, and he bounced up and down on his bottom in pure delight.

I reached forward again, but this time with gentleness and tenderness. And as I did up his buttons, I spoke to him softly and looked, for the first time, at the little boy. I looked into his eyes, which were bright and alert and full of mischief, and my heart went out to him.

It is strange, don't you think, how easily laughter can dispel fear?

Seeing these children with their small deformed bodies had brought home to me the stark realization of my own vulnerability. It was a reminder to me of how easily twisted and mangled, disabled, both physically and mentally, any of us can become.

And I had been afraid. Afraid to face the frailty of humankind. My own frailty.

God knows that every time I am reminded of my initial attitude toward these children, I feel a wave of shame wash over me. My lack of understanding and compassion and my inability to look farther than my own self is something I will always be ashamed of.

How much more ugly was I in my intolerance of imperfection than that small boy, ugly in appearance but undoubtedly pure in heart? Tenfold, I think.

David's mind had grasped most things while he was on this side, even though it had been impossible for him to reveal that in a physical way.

Now here was his opportunity to show his mother just exactly how much he had been aware of and how much he had understood when he had been on this side.

Initially Mrs. Harrison found it hard to respond to her son's first attempts at communication from beyond the grave. But she soon overcame her nervousness, and then David's comments had her smiling and relaxed. He amazed his mother by his directness and confidence and by his ability to communicate. She understood everything he said, and the evidence he gave of his survival was phenomenally accurate.

There were a few tears at this reunion, both from David and his mum, but they were tears of pure joy, not of sadness.

Then, toward the end of the sitting, David had this to say: "My mum, my dad, and my sister used to tell me every day just how much they loved me. I would sit in my wheelchair, or on the settee in my special place, and listen to the words of love and reassurance which they constantly gave to me. Even though they were not sure whether I could hear or understand, it made no difference. They told me just the same.

"It was impossible for me to respond to them in any way, as

I simply could not move a muscle. But my mind reached out to them in the hope that they could hear me—a boy locked away in a prison.

"I couldn't walk, I couldn't talk, I couldn't run or shout or play football. But those things don't matter anymore. Tell my mum, Rosemary, please, that I can walk now, that I can run and play and do all the things she always hoped I would one day be able to do. In all my life on the earth plane, my mum was there for me. Caring, loving, gentle. Tell her, please, that I can talk now, and tell her, please, Rosemary, 'I love, you, Mum.'

"My life," he continued, "goes on in the spirit world, and I learn and grow, but I will always be there for my mum, as she was for me, whenever she needs me."

I have seen June Harrison and her husband many times since that first sitting and have come to know David very well. And believe it or not, he often comes with me when I go out to give public demonstrations, and he is able from time to time to help with my work. After all those years of doing nothing, this young man is now very active and is helping people wherever he can. But I do remember one occasion when David came to help and that help became just a little embarrassing for me.

I was a guest speaker at a special dinner held at a hotel in Newcastle, which is in the north of England. Around 150 people were there, and after talking to them for a while I decided that I would demonstrate spirit communication. I had been aware of David's presence since the evening had begun (I had been talking to his mother earlier that same day), but now as I looked at my audience, I saw him standing by one of the tables, laughing and pointing to one of the gentlemen sitting there.

"Come over here," David called to me. "His name's David, too . . . his gran is here to talk to him."

Dutifully I approached the table and asked the man, "Is your name David?" He said yes, it was, and having spotted his grandmother standing next to "my David," I proceeded to give him a message from her that he understood totally.

So far so good; the evening was progressing as it should. I had promised David that he could help, and he had taken me at my word, so he went from table to table, indicating to me the next and then the next recipient of messages from those in the spirit world. The problem was that David had decided that the only people to get a message this night were those who bore the name of David or who had husbands or sons by that name. You can imagine that I gave the name of David so often that it became much too repetitious; but I had made a promise and had to stick by it. Fortunately, once I had explained to the audience what was happening, that David liked his name so much, and also liked the idea of being in charge, they thought it was almost as funny as David did . . . and he thought it was hilarious. I found it funny, too, eventually, and I thank God for the day that this young man came into my life.

David is one of my favorite people, and his story tells it all. The end of his life on this side came when he developed a chest infection. His tiny body was too frail, too weak, to fight it, and he "died."

But the boy survived and has gone on to become a man, strong, compassionate, and caring. He has fought his battle, and he has won.

And with God's help, so shall we all.

The
Girl

How old was she? Three, perhaps, or possibly four years old. The bed, pushed into the corner of the bedroom, seemed, even if only temporarily, a safe harbor.

She sat, huddled into the farthest corner, underneath. A tiny creature, so frail, just a young thing, and afraid. If she stayed quiet, maybe they would forget that she was there.

She listened as they argued. Her mother yelling at her father, "You'll kill her if you're not careful. For God's sake, man, leave her be."

And her father: "Move away, woman, and let me get my hands on the little brat."

He had beaten her all the way up the stairs and into the bedroom, and in desperation she had sought refuge under the bed.

Trembling and fearful, the girl stared up at the springs of

the bed. They seemed so large compared with her small frame and became imprinted on her memory.

The arguing continued for quite some time, an eternity, it seemed; then, quite suddenly, all was quiet.

This sudden stillness was more frightening than all that had gone on before, and the girl sat still, hardly daring to breathe in case "they" heard her. And she waited.

She didn't know what she had done to provoke such action on the part of her father. She only knew that he might kill her if she made even one sound. So she didn't cry, and she didn't move. She just sat as still as she possibly could.

Then, without warning, an arm reached out under the bed and grabbed her, hauling her unceremoniously into the middle of the room and dragging her down the stairs and out into the street.

The girl, still too scared to make even one sound, gazed up at her mother's furious face. The fierce grip of her mother's fingers tightened around her arm, and she was almost carried along to the top of the street and into a stranger's house.

"Keep her here, will you?" said the girl's mother with icy calm. "If he sets eyes on her once more today, he'll kill her for sure."

The girl looked at the small group of women gathered in the kitchen of the house she was now in. She had never seen them before, but obviously her mother knew them. They didn't say a word but, tight-lipped, nodded their agreement.

With that, the girl's mother turned on her heel and was gone.

Not a word, or a smile, or even a reassuring look toward her small daughter. No affection, no warmth, just emptiness.

This was to become the pattern of the girl's life. Not always being dragged to a neighbor's house, often having to stay and face the consequences of whatever terrible deed she was supposed to have done. And rarely knowing what it was that was to evoke such anger, not only in her father, but in her mother, too.

Her sisters got into trouble sometimes and were smacked, but they were never really beaten as she was.

Midge was her favorite sister, but Midge was also her mother's favorite daughter. There were only eighteen months between them, but Midge was considered the baby of the family.

The two older sisters, Audrey and Judy, were encouraged by their mother to favor the baby and to ridicule the girl, as was the whole family.

The girl, very sensitive and aware more and more as she grew up of her mother's dislike of her, began to build barriers. But that only made matters worse, as she was then thought sullen and moody, as well as a crybaby.

How many times had she heard her mother or father snap, "And you can take that look off your face, young lady"?

When there was any trouble in the house the girl's parents would summon their daughters into the living room. There, her father would tell them all what it was that had gone wrong and ask who was responsible. Of course, there would follow the inevitable silence, as none of the sisters would be prepared to own up. They all knew the consequences.

Their father would then say, "All right, go and sit on the stairs. Talk it out amongst yourselves and decide which of you is guilty. You can have ten minutes."

This was always the way, and often as the sisters were filing out of the door the mother would prod the girl hard in the back with her finger, saying, "And we both know which one of you it is."

The girl stood no chance, guilty or not, and when, after the ten minutes were up, the sisters filed back into the room, all denying whatever wrongdoing it was, more often than not her father would look straight at her and, in the voice she had come to dread, would say, "Go upstairs, take your pants off, lean over the bed, and wait for me to come up."

Silently the girl would climb the stairs, biting down hard on her bottom lip, trying not to cry, terrified of the pain that was to come.

Sometimes her father would come upstairs within a few minutes, but more often than not he would make her wait, knowing that the waiting was the hardest part of the punishment.

Whether he took half an hour or an hour, it made no difference to the girl. She would lie, trembling, half over the bed, facedown in the bedclothes, with her bare bottom exposed and ready for the smacking she knew was to come. She would stand rigid, not daring to move in case he came up and caught her out. Even if she was desperate for the toilet, her fear of her father was such that she dared not move.

The severity of the smacking would depend on the father's mood, but again, often he would take his time about it. His hands, hard and unyielding, would come down again and again on the child's small bottom, sharp and stinging, causing her to scream out over and over.

Afterward, she would be left sobbing on the bed, her backside scarlet and the pain in her back almost unbearable.

Her mother's hands were hard, too, but were more often used in temper. How many times did her mother's hand swing across hard to land the girl a violent slap across the face? The girl would have found it impossible to count. But her mother's sharp tongue was much much worse and, to the girl, far more painful.

When the girl was five, she was taken with her sisters on a fortnight's holiday to the seaside by their mother and her boyfriend (their father was away in the army at this time), whom the girls were told by their mother to call "Uncle." The girls came to know a few "uncles" over the years while their father was away, but never really very well, as they would come and go.

It should have been a happy time; after all, most kids like to paddle and play in the sand. But the girl was frightened of the waves and the noise that the sea made. It seemed to her to be coming to swallow her up. Everything would have been fine, though, if only her mother had been content to let her play quietly on the sand. But no, this just wasn't good enough, the girl's mother decided, so:

The girl was carried by the "uncle" to the very edge of the sea and made to sit on the cold muddy sand, screaming and crying as the waves washed over her legs.

The three sisters were left to play happily on the beach, and Mother and "Uncle" sat well away from the girl so as not to be disturbed too much by the girl's cries.

Ages passed, and what seemed like a lifetime later, the girl, now red-faced and still screaming in terror, saw the uncle ambling slowly toward her.

He reached down to pick her up, and thinking that he had come to rescue her, she reached out her tiny arms to him in desperate relief. But before she knew what was happening, he swung her up and, cradling her tightly in his arms so that she could hardly breathe, walked with her into the sea.

The girl opened her mouth to let out yet another terrified scream but was silenced by the huge wave that crashed over her small body, as the "uncle" dipped her into the sea.

How long he played this game, it was impossible to say—waiting for the waves to come and dipping the girl under again and again, almost drowning her in the process. When, finally, he brought her out of the sea and dropped her, choking and coughing, onto the beach, she was told, "That'll teach you for being a crybaby."

Where were her mother's arms to hold and comfort her? Where was her mother's love?

The girl grew to midteens, and nothing much had changed in her life. Her birthdays had come and gone with no excitements, but she had become more stubborn and more withdrawn. She looked often at her life and tried to find and remember the nice times. There must have been some, mustn't there, if she thought hard enough?

What about the time when she was six and the family had moved to Germany for a year? It was Christmas, and her mother had been in hospital. It was the first time they had spent a Christmas with just their father. And Santa had brought her a teddy bear. She was perhaps too old at six to have got her first teddy, but to the girl he was something to love, something to cuddle, and someone to hold tight to in the night when she was afraid.

And her father had been different, nice, funny, and Christmas had been good.

Then there was the time, still in Germany, when the girl was awakened suddenly by the loud crashing of thunder. She sat bolt upright in bed, trembling and frightened, as lightning flashed and more thunder crashed and crackled ominously across the sky. It was only as she looked around for her sisters, who all shared the same large bedroom, and realized that they weren't there and that she was all alone, that the girl began to cry.

Just as she had begun to think that everyone had left and that the house was empty, unexpectedly her father appeared in the doorway. What was she more afraid of, him or the storm that raged outside? She was only six years old and already so afraid of life.

But to her amazement, her father wasn't cross with her, and as he sat on the bed and talked to her, he held her tiny hand.

"It's only a silly old storm," he said, "and your sisters have gone downstairs, crying and afraid, but we're not, are we now?"

The girl gazed into her father's face and heard his voice, gentle and soothing, and tentatively she shook her head. "Now lie down," continued her father, "and we'll see how close the storm is."

And they stayed together in the darkened room, waiting for the lightning, then counting slowly until the thunder came. The longer the count between the thunder and lightning, the farther away from them was the storm.

The girl's father had turned it into a game. But it was a game that only the two of them could play. It was exciting, special, and the girl felt safe.

She couldn't remember how long he stayed. It must have been until she had fallen asleep, as the next thing she knew it was morning and the storm had gone.

But she could remember that for the first time in her young life, she and her father had shared a precious moment. He had seemed to care.

She could also remember the time when she was in the children's home and it was her birthday.

All the children had come down into the big hall for breakfast, and the girl was asked to stand up while everyone sang "Happy Birthday" to her. That was nice, she recalled, but even nicer was when she was given the doll. It was a green rag doll, not very pretty, but it was the first birthday present she could ever remember getting, and she thought it was wonderful.

How old would she have been then? Seven or eight? The girl wasn't quite sure, as she had been put in the home twice. Why she had been put there she also wasn't sure about, as no one in the family talked about it, and if she asked, it might cause trouble. And everyone knew that the girl always caused trouble, didn't they?

Later, much later, the girl discovered that she had been put in the home because her mother had gone over to Germany to see her father, and there had been no one to look after her.

The girl's happiest memories were of the long school holidays when she was minded out to the most wonderful lady in the world. She was told to call her Auntie Loseby, although she was no relation at all.

Auntie Loseby took to the girl, recognizing in her that gentle sensitivity of most lost children. During those holidays, even though they didn't last, the girl blossomed like a rose in summer. She was spoiled, not only by the old lady, but by her son, Uncle Tony, as the girl called him, and by his wife, Auntie Sheena.

Every Sunday they had a proper tea, all laid out on the table. The girl would sometimes stand and gaze in open admiration at the splendor of it.

The three adults, after bustling the girl onto her chair,

would then sit quietly, with knowing looks and secret smiles, waiting for the game to begin.

It was always the same, and the girl loved it.

Shyly she would lift her eyes to examine the goodies on the table, looking to see if Auntie Loseby had made her very favorite thing. No, she couldn't see it, it wasn't there, and the girl was far too shy to mention it.

She would wriggle a little on her seat and wonder if perhaps this time her auntie Loseby had actually not remembered.

But then Uncle Tony would exclaim in mock horror, "No lemon curd tarts today, Mum? Oh no, don't tell me you've forgotten!"

The girl would giggle and blush scarlet with embarrassment while staring intently at her feet, too shy to say anything or even to look at anyone.

Auntie Loseby, also playing the game to the full, would then exclaim in a puzzled voice, "But I put them on the table, I'm sure I did. You haven't eaten them all, Tony, have you?"

Sometimes the game would last for ages but would always end with Uncle Tony producing a huge plate of delicious-looking lemon curd tarts from somewhere underneath the table. And he always managed to do this with a great flourish, a wicked grin, and a wonderful twinkle in his eyes.

Then, on one of her visits to this lovely household, Auntie Loseby told the girl that Aunt Sheena was going to have a baby. This was wonderful news for all of them, but it meant that there would be no room now for the girl. There could be no more visits or long stays during the school holidays. But the girl had her memories, which she treasured.

More years passed, and the girl grew taller but remained very thin. Her sisters, even Midge, the youngest, grew out as well as up. They developed curves in all the right places, wore bras, started their periods "on time"; in fact, they were happy, healthy, "normal" young ladies.

The girl's mother made sure that she, the girl, realized what an ugly duckling she was by comparison. It was pointed out on numerous occasions that she was pigeon chested, had no shape, no meat on her arms or her skinny little legs. The other girls were encouraged to laugh and ridicule, which they did, and the girl felt more and more inadequate.

Still, though, there remained in her that spark of independence and a stubborn refusal to lie down and die. She still laughed, still played with her dolls, Jennifer and Susan, and of course her teddy, living in the make-believe world she had now created for herself. A world of make-believe friends—a world of love.

Of course, there were good times, and there were the times when the sisters played together and had fun. When she was eleven or twelve the girl's older brother, Terry, started going out with a young woman who was a music teacher, so piano lessons were arranged for her. This was great, as the girl showed a certain aptitude and found yet another way of escaping the real world when things at home weren't right.

She would sit for hours in the front room and play. Hardly anyone came in to disturb her, as the room was cold, even in the summer. In winter it was freezing, and she would sit, well wrapped up in a coat and scarf, oblivious of everything around her save her music. Not by anyone's standards could the girl be considered a brilliant pianist. Sometimes well, sometimes clumsily, her fingers would embrace the keyboard, but her thoughts were set free and she could express herself in a way she never could with words. And her parents, although they never were especially encouraging, never discouraged her.

But when she was fifteen, something happened that almost destroyed any ability she might have had to remember with affection the good times she must undoubtedly have had in her childhood.

The family were on holiday again, this time in Ireland and also this time with her father.

The four sisters had gone to the local village dance, but Judy and Midge decided halfway through the evening that they were bored and went home. The girl would quite willingly have gone with them, but Audrey, the eldest, persuaded her to stay. Audrey was nineteen and having a great time. The young Irishman dancing her around the floor was very handsome.

Eventually the dance finished, and the young man asked if he could walk her home. Of course she said yes, but she persuaded the girl to act as chaperone.

Soon they reached the house where the family were staying for their holiday, and the girl was all for going straight in. But Audrey wanted to stay and talk to the boy, so again the girl was persuaded to wait with her, and was told to stand a few feet away from her sister—near enough for protection, but not close enough to hear what her sister and the boy might say to each other.

Ten uneventful minutes passed, and the girl was just beginning to get fidgety and on the point of telling her sister that she was going in, when the door of the house flew open, and out stepped the girl's father.

In an instant she froze, some instinct telling her of danger. Then his great bellowing voice, like black thunder rolling across the street, moved both sisters into action, and they raced into the house.

"Get yourselves in," he had roared, that was all. Just three words, but the girl felt the rage that lay behind them, and her stomach lurched in fear and dread of what would happen next.

Audrey reached the door first, and her father's hand came out expertly to give her a resounding clout across the head.

Close on her heels came the girl, who also received a sound blow across her head. But it didn't stop there.

All the way up the stairs she was beaten soundly by her father. They reached the upstairs living room, but still he didn't stop. Somehow, with blows raining down on her thick and fast, the girl managed to get to the bedroom and tried to protect herself by curling into a ball on the bed.

Audrey had been screaming and yelling at her father to leave the girl alone (it was the first time the girl could ever remember anyone trying to help her), and then Audrey jumped onto her father's back in an attempt to pull him away.

With one raging sweep of his hand he flung her off, and she landed with a thud in the corner of the room, tears of rage and frustration pouring down her face.

He drew his attention back to the girl huddled on the bed, her arms trying to protect her face and head, and he beat her and beat her until eventually his rage was spent.

She had long since stopped screaming out and had lain shocked and numb as her father's fists had thudded down on her thin and narrow frame. It seemed to her later that only one thing had registered in her mind. At one point, somewhere in all this, she had looked desperately for her mother and had seen her standing with her other two sisters in the doorway to the bedroom, watching. Just watching. She didn't move, or speak, or yell out for this barbaric act to stop. Nor, when it eventually did stop, did she lift one finger to help the girl in any way. She just turned on her heel, taking her three daughters with her, and the girl was left once again by herself, and all alone.

Why, you may ask, was the girl beaten this way? Why? Why?

The girl's father may know, or maybe he doesn't, and her mother may have an inkling as to why.

But the girl never knew!

Years passed, and the girl, now a woman but still a girl, shy, sensitive, and self-conscious, was married.

Would her life become easier now that she had found someone to love and who loved her? Well, he did, didn't he? Even though, just two days before the wedding, he had been to bed with another woman.

But it seemed that the girl was fated, as only a few months after she was married, illness struck. She was rushed to the hospital, desperately ill with what at first the doctors thought was some sort of viral kidney infection. It turned out to be much worse, but after two rounds of major surgery and lots of care from the medical profession, the girl slowly recovered her health.

During all the months of her illness, she had just one visit from her eldest sister, Audrey, and one from her mother. There were no cards or flowers or phone messages. Nothing to show the girl that her family cared.

She could have died, but what would it have mattered to them?

Nothing, she felt, just nothing!

So she clung more and more to her husband, needing him to fill the desperate loneliness that was her soul.

She lost her first baby, and her second, and can remember coming round from the anesthetic after they had scraped her clean, screaming for her baby. But an injection soon sorted that out, and after a long sleep she woke to find that physically she could cope. It was only her mind that screamed out now. Why? Why? *Why?*

Years passed, and her third baby was born, a girl. She was well and healthy and became the girl's salvation.

Twice her husband left her, once with the girl's best friend. There were always other women, always debts, always problems of one sort or another. But the girl had grown dependent on her husband, believing firmly in her own inadequacy and her inability to manage without him.

Twice she took him back, willing to believe him when he told her that it was only her he loved. In fairness, he probably meant it at the time, or at least for the time it took him to say the words.

During this period, the girl, from time to time, would invite her parents to visit, always hoping that somehow they would be able to build up some kind of loving relationship.

Strangely, since the girl had left home, she and her father got on very well, and a certain kind of closeness developed between them. They found that they could talk to each other and were on the same wavelength. Never once did either of them mention the past or even refer to the bad times. But the girl felt that her father had finally come to accept and even care for her. She in turn began to understand that her father was not a wicked man, merely a frustrated and unhappy man, living in a marriage he did not want and with a woman too complex to ever understand. He had tried, she had tried, but their marriage was an unmitigated disaster. And since the kids had left home they began to live more and more separate lives, he in his garden and the girl's mother taking holidays abroad, cruises, and visiting her daughters. It was probably her mother's absence from home that enabled the girl to get to know her father better and to grow to like him as well as to love him. This did not mean that she could forget the past, the beatings and the cruelty, and it took a number of years for her to come to terms with this aspect of her relationship with him. But just as things between them were going really well, fate struck yet another cruel blow. The girl's father, the army sergeant, had a massive heart attack and died.

How the girl grieved. She grieved for the loss of her daddy, for the fact that she hadn't said good-bye and that she wouldn't see him again. She grieved for the hurts and pains of the past and for all the lost opportunities. For the love she could have had and for the love she had had. And she grieved most of all for all those might-have-beens.

But the pain lessened, as most pain does with time, and the girl learned through it all that her parents really meant a great deal to her. She resolved to try harder with her mother and began to hope, as her mother visited her more often, that they too could develop some sort of loving or close relationship.

But on one of these visits it was made perfectly plain to her that this could never be.

They were in the kitchen, the girl busy preparing dinner and her mother full of talk about the cruise she had just been on. Peeling potatoes, the girl listened, half amused, to her mother's tales of the man she had met on the ship. With thorough enthusiasm her mother recounted, word for word, all that he had said to her and all that she had said to him.

The girl nodded and murmured in all the right places as her mother prattled on and on. But then something she said froze the smile on the girl's face, and time seemed to stand still.

"Well, I told him all about the house," the girl heard her say, "and all about my lovely garden, and the dahlias, and of course," she went on, hardly stopping for breath, "I told him all about my three lovely daughters."

Not only was the smile on the girl's face frozen, but her hands, poised wet and dripping over the potatoes, never moved; her whole body seemed suspended, waiting, waiting, for what?

Had her mother really said that? Could she have misheard? But no, she knew that she had not, and her mother's words seemed to bounce about inside her head, over and over.

And I told him about my three lovely daughters . . . three lovely daughters . . . three lovely daughters . . .

But her mother had four daughters, hadn't she?

As soon as the words were out of the older woman's mouth, she realized what she had said, and for a few brief seconds she also froze. Then, with a shrug of her shoulders and an impatient wave of her hand toward the girl, she stated matter-of-factly: "Well, you and I have never been close, have we?"

The girl didn't speak. She couldn't speak. The lump in her throat was threatening to choke her. Suddenly she came alive again and jumped into action. Furiously she chopped vegetables, made pastry, mixed gravy.

Her mother, oblivious of the girl's feelings, prattled on and on about her wonderful cruise.

The tight band of pain, so familiar now, closed around the girl's chest, and she felt the sharp stinging behind her eyes as the tears tried to push their way out. Oh, God, no! she cried out silently. Please don't let me cry. Don't let her see my tears, dear God, please don't let her see my pain.

Her mother didn't want her. Nor did her family; nor, it seemed, did her husband. Why? Was she so repellent, so awful to be around, so terrible to live with? Why, she questioned, did everyone she love reject her, and so terribly?

It was hard sometimes to stop the fierce feelings of self-pity from engulfing her completely, especially at the time when her marriage broke down and she was left penniless and alone.

But somehow, from somewhere deep within her, the girl found an inner strength, and she fought her loneliness and her despair. This was not an easy task, but the girl's character was strong, and her ability to laugh and her capacity to love saw her through.

She came to realize that not everyone she loved had rejected her. In fact, the one person in her life she loved the most, her daughter, had been her strength, her support, and at times her only reason for living. Even then the girl came to realize that she must not rely on her daughter too much but learn to go forward in life for herself as well. And she knew that if she wanted to grow, then it was up to her. No one else could do it for her, only she could help herself.

There is an old but true saying: "God helps those who help themselves." It was up to her to make the effort, and in doing so, the girl knew that she would have the guidance and support from God that she so desperately needed. Strangely, her faith in Him had never wavered, even in the times she had doubted herself the most, she had never doubted God's love for her. Despite her faults and failings, the girl knew in her heart that God loved her. And through Him she finally began to see clearly her purpose in life.

There are many kinds of pain that we on this earth plane are forced to experience. The girl's pain and suffering is nothing compared to the suffering of a parent forced to face the loss of their child. This kind of pain must surely be the worst to bear.

But any kind of suffering is a lesson, and we can choose to learn and grow or not, as we wish.

Through her pain, the girl learned a little and developed within herself compassion and sensitivity for the grief of others.

In writing this chapter, the girl has had to face many memories, and tears of pain, grief, and sorrow have been shed upon these pages. The telling of this story has been, to say the least, hard. But in looking back on her life, the girl in all truth can say she wouldn't change one thing. She knows that all those hurtful and painful memories, combined with the many joyful ones, have molded her into what she is today.

The medium, strong, laughing, happy, sits in the sun, her daughter, Samantha, by her side, her dog, Karma, at her feet. She can look with compassion into the eyes and hearts of all who seek her help. And with true feeling for their hurts and for their pain can say, "I understand."

The girl has grown into a woman.

The rose has blossomed.

This is my story, this is my life. In so many ways it is no different from most. The pains and hurts, the joys and moments of happiness, even if for different reasons, are similar to many others. In other ways my story, my life, is vastly different, and many of my experiences are unbelievable.

I could say that I am as ordinary as the next man or woman ... knowing that when God gave us His miracle, which is LIFE, He knew that we are, all of us, anything but ordinary.

Every one of us has a story to tell, for our lives are unrehearsed, like a play, a drama, or a movie. Each life, no matter how long or short, is a gift, God given, given for a purpose ... that purpose the enhancement of the soul, for the soul's purpose is to learn, to grow.

When we give life, create a life, then we create a miracle. When we give meaning to that life, learning not to judge, trying to find forgiveness in our hearts for those who did harm to us, then we create an even bigger miracle. But when we give life to our own selves, forgiving the harm we do to our own selves, to give meaning and purpose to our own lives, then God must surely smile, knowing that His gift to us has been valued. And that must be the greatest miracle of all.

My miracle is my life.

My miracle is all life.

My miracle is life after life.

My miracle is my child's life.

My miracle is that each and every one of us has a miracle ... is a miracle.

And I look to my guide, Grey Eagle, my teacher, my friend, and I ask, What can we do for each other? How do we nurture our world? How do we bring light into our lives?

His eyes kind and full of understanding and love ... he answers ... With GENTLENESS ... and only with GENTLENESS.

Epilogue

There are many things I have to tell you, much information I have to impart, about the spirit world, and the people of the spirit world. In the next book I must tell you more of their story, and how we—we who live on this Earth plane—how our actions, our thoughts, create reactions in the world of spirit.

There is much to tell, and much to teach, and, as Grey Eagle would say, come sit with me . . . draw close to me now . . . past the beginning . . . let me tell you more of my journey, of my travels to the Far East, and of how I came to America.

Come sit with me . . . draw close to my fire . . . warm your hands . . . and I will continue my story.

I am a medium now, full fledged, flying high. Having experienced so very much I am no longer uncertain of my life, my work. With great confidence, born of an even greater faith, I tread my path—Grey Eagle, ever watchful, by my side.

It was July 1992, and although I had never intended, indeed never had any inclination to visit America, here I was.

It was hard to believe that just a few months before I had been in Hong Kong visiting an American friend, Lynne, and we had planned this trip.

In fact it was Lynne's suggestion that we tour the American West beginning in New Mexico—Santa Fe to be exact—and slowly working our way round to Phoenix, Arizona.

My first and most major concern when this idea was broached was financial. Could I afford it? The answer came back loud and clear: *no*, I could not. But as my friend and I sat poring over the map, discussing the possible route we would take I caught sight of the place I needed to visit: Apache Country.

I looked more closely at the map. "The White Mountains," "Fort Apache," "Apache Territory," and Phoenix . . . *Phoenix*. I traced a line with my finger, no doubt in my mind. I heard the mountains calling me, calling me home.

This was an adventure, and I was excited. Grey Eagle was bringing me back to his homeland—bringing me back. Santa Fe was charming, the Grand Canyon spectacular, Phoenix and our stay in a dome house . . . well, I'll tell you more of these things later.

And so we close the final pages of this book only to discover that we have opened the first pages of another.

If you are interested in learning more about Rosemary
Altea and her work, you can visit her website at
www.rosemaryaltea.com
or write to her at
Rosemary Altea, P.O. Box 1151, Manchester, VT 05254